Growing Up in
Bloody Mingo
West Virginia

by
Andrew Chafin

HERITAGE BOOKS
2008

HERITAGE BOOKS

AN IMPRINT OF HERITAGE BOOKS, INC.

Books, CDs, and more—Worldwide

For our listing of thousands of titles see our website
at
www.HeritageBooks.com

Published 2008 by
HERITAGE BOOKS, INC.
Publishing Division
100 Railroad Ave. #104
Westminster, Maryland 21157

International Standard Book Numbers
Paperbound: 978-0-7884-2475-5
Clothbound: 978-0-7884-7323-4

To All Appalachians, Wherever You Are

The stereotype that Appalachians are backward, isolated, gap-toothed, moonshine-guzzling, uneducated inbred hillbillies always makes me want to draw my sword in defense of the warm-hearted, patriotic, friendly, hard-working, intelligent people who live in the tall, proud majestic mountains of Appalachia.

ANDREW CHAFIN

Acknowledgments

MANY OF THE GEOGRAPHIC and economic descriptions herein were taken or adapted from various reports of the Appalachian Regional Commission. Various books on the Hatfield-McCoy Feud were used as resource material.

Growing Up in Bloody Mingo was written as a history of my childhood for my children. I had planned to leave it for them upon my departure from this life.

Although my childhood was not unique, in that thousands of Appalachian children experienced similar childhoods, the place where I was born and raised always held a fascination for me. Mingo County, the Hatfields and McCoys, the Matewan Massacre and the coalmine wars were quite unique and a lively part of American history.

In the spring of 2002, I let my friend Patty Nichols read the book and she insisted it should be submitted to a publisher. I thank Patty for the encouragement she offered and all the work she did in getting the manuscript to a publisher.

And, finally, thanks to the Appalachian people who inspire me daily with their patriotism and friendship. I am proud to be one of them.

The Roots

MY GREAT, GREAT, GREAT GRANDFATHER, Valentine Hatfield
was born in Russell County, Virginia in the late 1700's. He
married Elizabeth Vance, also a native of the county, and they
produced eight boys and three girls.

After migrating to western Virginia, Elizabeth gave birth to
my great, great grandfather Ephraim in Logan County in 1812.
He was called "Big Eaf" and was said to be a huge and powerful man.

Big Eaf, on an apparent trip back to the homeplace, married
Nancy Vance of Russell County and they produced eighteen
children, two of whom were my great grandfather Ellison and
his brother, my great-great uncle Anderson who would come
to be known as "Devil Anse."

Ellison was killed violently by the McCoys in August 1882
on the election grounds across the river in Kentucky near
Matewan. Some say the killing of my great grandfather was
the catalyst that started the Hatfield-McCoy Feud.

Prior to Ellison's death he fathered my grandmother Lydia
who married Allen Chafin, the son of Moses Chafin, who was
the son of Nathan Chafin. My grandparents produced eight
daughters and three sons, one of whom was my father, Tom C.
Chafin.

My father married Hazel Isaac and they produced three sons and two daughters. I was the first of the five and was born in January 1937.

When I was six years old, I began to ask my dad, Tom, to tell me stories about the Hatfield-McCoy Feud. He brought the stories to life for me and they became an integral part of my childhood.

Although I would read many articles and books about the feud I always preferred my dad's version because as a child he often visited Devil Anse, and on one visit Devil gave him a dog named Black Bart. I felt his versions were more accurate because of this personal relationship.

The story of the Hatfield-McCoy feud fascinated me from the time I was a young boy. Later, as a teenager, I felt a sense of pride that my ancestors had made American history.

The feud was more than a fight between two families that only touched a few lives on the borders of West Virginia and Kentucky.

It was more than a lawsuit between Floyd Hatfield, a cousin of Devil Anse, and Randolph McCoy over the ownership of a hog.

It was more than the fabled romance between Johnse Hatfield and Roseanna McCoy and it was more than the three McCoy brothers killing my great grandfather Ellison on the election grounds in 1882.

It was all these and much more as it developed from a legal dispute involving two states all the way to the United States Supreme Court.

My childhood was consumed with memories of my ancestors and although my personal childhood adventures were exciting and adventuresome, always in the back of my mind were the shadowed figures of Great Grandfather Ellison and Great-great Uncle Devil Anse.

They were my heritage and always I yearned to live in their time and take up arms against the McCoys.

Introduction

IF YOU'RE READING THIS it's a pretty sure bet you had a child-hood. It's also a good bet that from time to time you reflect upon your childhood, and, whether it was good or bad or happy or sad, it was a special time in your journey through life and will remain in your memory as long as you live.

Growing Up in Bloody Mingo, a story of my childhood, is my special time and has been in my mind for forty years, in my bottom desk drawer for the past ten and in my heart forever.

When I was old enough to read I became concerned that newsmen and social scientists were calling Appalachia, "the land that time forgot" and referring to the Tug Fork of the Big Sandy River as the urinary tract of the mountains located in an area of social and political blight without parallel in the nation.

As a child I resented such characterizations of the place where I lived and I still resent it, but, as I grew older I became accustomed to the fact that the outside world regarded my Hatfield ancestors as bloody feudists, Mingo County and its coal miners as ignorant, uneducated hillbillies and central Appalachia as a backward, remote area far from the mainstream of American life.

My journey begins as I enter the first grade at New Town Elementary School and continues through my senior year at

Magnolia High School in Matewan, West Virginia, home of the Hatfields and McCoys and the Matewan Massacre.

The journey was filled with tears, hope, sorrow, love, happiness, boredom, excitement, adventure, pitfalls, opportunities, and an ever-awareness of my ancestry, all abundantly available in the land that time forgot.

Left to right: Andrew Chafin, Georgia Ann Chafin, Donald Ray Chafin, Tyrone Chafin. (Author's collection.)

One

WHEN I WAS SIX YEARS OLD, the population of New Town, a small, unincorporated, coal-mining community seven miles from Matewan in Mingo County, West Virginia, was home to 287 registered voters, thirty-seven cows, fourteen horses, two idiots and assorted dogs and cats, most of whom dressed up and came out on Saturday night to the Fuzzy Duck, the only beer joint in New Town.

Of the 287 voters, 253 were registered Democrats, 33 were Republicans, (the two idiots were in this group) and one was beyond classification.

Rumors that the dogs and cats were registered Democrats and voted via absentee ballots were unfounded except, perhaps, in several precincts at the lower end of the county.

About ninety of the registered Democrats had to be paid with cash or liquor or both before they would come to the polls and vote. But, they were honest. Once you bought them they stayed bought all day, refusing to sell out to the opposing side even at a higher price. It was a matter of honor.

The thirty-three Republicans, (other than the two idiots) couldn't be bought, but it didn't matter since they couldn't vote in the Democratic Primary and usually didn't have a Republican on the ballot anyway.

Matewan, better known as the land of the Hatfields and McCoys, and separated from Eastern Kentucky by the Tug Fork River, was a small town of cinderblock churches and brimstone preaching, which continually fought to share its narrow valley space with the Norfolk and Western Railroad and the Tug, a tributary of the Big Sandy River which flows into the Ohio River at Louisa, Kentucky.

Every two years or so, the Tug grew from a meek, harmless summer trickle into a vast, vengeful, devastating mountain of water determined to wipe out the town.

The townspeople prayed and patiently rebuilt, waited for the next flood and prayed and patiently rebuilt again until finally most of the town had washed away.

What remains today lies tranquil and unruffled beside the Tug River protected by a 2,350 foot long multi-million dollar floodwall, thanks primarily to United States Senator Robert C. Byrd, the King of Congressional Pork and West Virginia's greatest hero.

During the 1970's, newspaper and magazine writers began to find it fashionable to refer to Mingo County as the asshole of the world, located at the outermost limits of human civilization, no doubt because the county had produced such infamous characters as Smilin' Sid Hatfield, hero of the Matewan Massacre, Devil Anse Hatfield, leader of the Hatfield Clan which warred against the McCoys, and a host of other lesser known but equally bad outlaws and varmints who made up my family tree.

Being born in Mingo and having spent the first twenty-five years of my life there, I resented muckraking, low-life outsiders referring to my hometown as the asshole of the world, located at the edge of the universe.

And I still cringe when they call Tug River the urinary track of the mountains, Mingo County the hellhole of creation, and refer to my great uncle Devil Anse as a vicious, murdering varmint.

While birthright gives me leeway to cuss Matewan and Bloody Mingo, I find my backside puckering up when outsiders do it. Home is home and while Mingo county may not be the center of American culture, it's still home to me and has a special place in my heart.

Memories of my childhood began resurfacing in June 1988 when I learned the Matewan High School classes of 1954 through 1959 were having a thirty-year class reunion in late August.

Coming on the heels of John Sayles movie, "Matewan," which had already whetted my appetite to return to my roots, the upcoming reunion welled up a longing to see my kinfolk and classmates of yesteryear.

It seemed everybody who held an elective office was under indictment. During the year, the sheriff, several high county officials and other political leaders had been indicted or tucked away in federal prisons. I felt lucky I had moved to Virginia a few years earlier.

Political hanky panky was as much a part of life in Mingo County as eating breakfast each morning. In fact, while I was growing up, I often reminded my dad, Tom, an eventual high sheriff of the county, to be sure to bury me in Mingo if I died before he did so I could remain active in politics.

Long-standing rumor had it that all my dead ancestors still voted in every election, and Tom, who would later become the alleged leader of the "political machine," had jokingly assured me on many occasions that it was appropriate since they all voted a straight Democratic ticket.

I admired Tom and listened intently to his stories. His nose was straight and sat between two keen brown eyes, which seemed to observe things I didn't readily see. He resembled my great-great uncle and his great-uncle Devil Anse Hatfield. Like Devil's, his nose tilted ever so slightly to the right.

For some reason, which started when I was very young, I called my parents by their first names, Tom and Hazel. My brothers and sisters would do the same. People thought it was strange, but it seemed natural to us. Neither Tom nor Hazel ever commented on it to me.

My dad was kin to the Hatfields and my mother was an Isaac. Her family, while not as infamous as the Hatfields, managed to hold their own when it came to impropriety.

When my Uncle Ray Isaac was discharged from the Navy after World War II, he opened the Spinning Wheel, a nightclub with a huge dancing floor. Girls came from all over the county to the popular New Town nightspot because it was a well-known fact that the boys from New Town were the best dancers in the county.

Uncle Ray, who had served on the *U.S.S. Indiana*, was my mom's brother. She had two other brothers, Tommy and Jack. When Jack got out of the Navy he came in for a short time, but soon went to Chicago where he disappeared and was never heard from again. Rumors that he was killed by the Mob circulated throughout the community for years, but no one ever knew for sure what Uncle Jack's fate had been.

Uncle Ray had a small room off the back of the Spinning Wheel, which was used for illegal poker games. He sometimes let me act as house man. The house man didn't play, but cut the pot an appropriate amount after each game. The cut would go into a little hole on the middle of a cigar box and one night after a long game the box was almost full. I took it to Ray and he pulled a twenty-dollar bill out of the box and gave it to me. That was a lot of money. Beer was only a quarter and RC Cola only a dime. Twenty would last a long time.

As the reunion drew near, the long, hot dry days of August passed slowly. My thoughts were increasingly invaded with memories of my carefree childhood days along the banks of Mate Creek and Tug River.

I hoped all my cousins would attend. It was hard to believe I hadn't seen some of them for more than thirty years.

Our distinguished careers began in the first grade in 1942. Our elementary school was a large, L-shaped, three-room frame building and the largest structure in the community. The school accommodated grades one through six, had three teachers and one unpainted outhouse. Inside the outhouse, two holes were cut in the elevated, wooden throne. Deciding which hole to use was always a constant annoyance. The simultaneous use of the holes was unthinkable.

Now, after forty-five years, I'm still embarrassed to tell the very first thing I remember at New Town Elementary, but the second thing I remember was dropping my pencil during writing class.

We were practicing our writing and the classroom was very quiet. It was a common enough experience, but as I reached under the desk to retrieve my pencil, I accidentally expelled a small burst of gas which my cousin Bo Chafin would later describe as a wet, weird, thunderous, black fart.

The desks, lined in neat little rows, were too small to crawl under so I had to come back up. The muffled snickers of my classmates seemed deafening to me, and I thought I detected a faint smile cross Miss Lee's face.

I was totally humiliated and felt sure I would never again be able to face my classmates with integrity. They forgot about it in a few days. I still remember.

My classmates in 1942 were mostly first cousins, second cousins, third cousins, and distant relatives. About half of us would be together for twelve years of school. The others would drop out and find work in the coal mines or move to Ohio whenever they could hitch a ride with a relative who had gone before and had come home for a long weekend visit.

Occasionally, someone would move away to look for a job, but no one ever moved into our small community. The only people who moved to New Town were those just getting born. The population stayed about the same because every time someone was born, someone else migrated to Ohio.

We were an isolated, close-knit group of kinsmen who fought each other often and violently, but rallied together whenever one of our own was beset upon by an outsider from across the mountain.

I considered an outsider to be anyone who lived outside a ten-mile stretch from Meador to Matewan. Once past those boundaries, it seemed to me to be a long way from home.

As a six-year old, I had become familiar with Matewan. I knew it was the scene of much of the Hatfield-McCoy Feud and whenever we went to town I always looked for Hatfields and McCoys.

Tom would point them out to me, but I was always disappointed they didn't have long beards and weren't carrying guns. The town seemed rather drab in light of all the menacing stories I had heard.

My first trip to Matewan with Tom was almost my last. We were in Tom's red pickup truck, which he used to haul one-hundred-pound sacks of cattle feed for resale at his small grocery store.

He pulled up to the feed store, which was separated from the backside of Matewan by three sets of railroad tracks. Somehow, we became separated in the store and I went back out to the truck.

Outside, I tried to walk the railroad track without falling off. When I turned back toward the feed store, I saw an old black man walking toward me. I knew instantly that it was Johnny Banks. I had heard Tom talk about Johnny Banks and I was terrified of him. Once when we were on our way to Matewan, my brother Don and I were fighting in the back seat. Tom turned to Hazel and said, "Let's stop the car and put them out and let Johnny Banks get them."

I either had to pass by him or run across the tracks.

It wouldn't have been a major decision if a coal train hadn't been coming around the bend, but I was more afraid of Johnny Banks than the train so I dashed across the tracks. I didn't get across by much.

When Tom came out of the feed store he began to search for me and I heard him calling for me. I'm sure he thought I had been run over by the train.

When the train finally passed I saw Tom standing by the truck and ran back across the tracks. I didn't say anything about Johnny Banks. I didn't want him to know I had been scared.

On our way back to New Town I asked, "Why did they call Devil Anse Devil? Was he really a mean man?"

"There was no more peaceful man in the mountains than Devil Anse," he answered.

"Then why did they call him the Devil," I countered, "if he was so peaceful?"

"Well, now, there's several stories and I'm not sure which one was right."

"What were the stories?" I asked.

"Well, now some say he got it after fighting off the Union soldiers on a high mountain over in Logan County called the Devil's Backbone. Others say that Aunt Levicy, his wife, called him meaner than the Devil after he had been in a scrape with a moonshiner and the name stuck, but I don't think anybody really knows how he got the nickname.

"It sure was a funny name for a peaceful man," I said. "Did Devil Anse really meet Frank James on the banks of the Tug River below Matewan," I asked, "or was that just a tall tale?"

"No, that was true," said Tom.

"What was James doing on the Tug?"

"Well, a few days before Devil and James met there was a big bank robbery in Huntington and everybody knew it was the James Gang."

"Was Jesse James with them?" I asked.

"No, Jesse wasn't with 'em."

"What did Devil say to Frank James?"

"Well, Devil was out hunting on a ridge down near Matewan when he saw a rider on the banks of the Tug. He knew the rider was no McCoy because his horse was shiny black and he had on a new nice-looking overcoat. No McCoy had such a horse or coat.

As Devil let his horse Fred, a thoroughbred of racing stock, descend the ridge slowly toward the Tug, he paused occasionally to listen as his keen eyes searched for additional riders. Satisfied the rider was alone he nudged Fred from behind a pawpaw bush.

"Howdy," the stranger said.

"Howdy," replied Devil.

"What was he doing by himself?" I asked.

"Well there was four men who robbed the bank and they split up and went separate ways," Tom replied.

"Did they ever catch 'em?" I asked.

"No, they never got 'em."

"What else did Devil say to James?" I asked.

"Well, it seems James was looking for a place to cross the river and he told him to go on up around the bend where the water was shallow."

"Did Devil know he was Frank James?"

"Not until he heard about the bank being robbed a few days later," he said.

"What really started the feud?" I asked.

"Well, now some say the trouble started during the Civil War. The McCoys fought for the North and the Hatfields for the South. Some say that the trouble started when Harmon McCoy, a brother of Randolph, was found dead in a cave near Devil Anse's house," he answered.

"Some say it started over the hog that Randolph McCoy claimed was stolen from him by Floyd Hatfield. I guess all of these things brought it on but when they killed my grandfather Ellison it just broke out into open warfare."

My second trip to Matewan was worse. One morning when I was eight, Tom awakened Don and me before daylight and got us out of bed. "Get up boys, we're going to buy a cow," he said.

We loaded up in the red truck and I asked why we had our pajamas on. Tom assured me it didn't matter because we would be back before breakfast.

In town we stopped at the Matewan Hospital and went in. I was soon on a table with someone holding an ether bag over my face and telling me to blow. We didn't get a cow but the Doctor got my tonsils.

I didn't know if Don was in on the plot or if he thought we were going to buy a cow.

My future trips to Matewan, which would in 1997 be designated a historical landmark by the National Park Service, could only get better.

"Devil Anse" Hatfield, leader of the clan. (Photo courtesy of Charlotte Sanders, *Williamson Daily News*, from the Gravely-Moore Studio Collection, West Virginia State Archives, Department of Culture and History, Charleston.]

TWO

THE WEST VIRGINIA LEGISLATURE created Mingo County in 1895 by bisecting Logan County, which had been in the Commonwealth of Virginia, one of the thirteen original colonies.

Logan County was named in honor of Tar-gar-jute, an Indian Chief who was called Logan after James Logan of Pennsylvania, who educated him.

In 1824, William Burgess, a member of the Virginia General Assembly, convinced legislators to make Logan a new county. It included the present counties of Logan, Wyoming, Mingo, Mercer, Raleigh, Fayette, Boone, Lincoln, Cabell, Kanawha and part of McDowell, and the Virginia counties of Tazewell and Giles, a vast and beautiful colonial empire.

The separation of the western counties created the new state of West Virginia in 1863, and in 1895 Mingo was created. The state's youngest county, Mingo got its name from the Mingo Indian tribe ruled by Chief Logan.

In the beginning the land was covered with beautiful green mountains, sprinkled abundantly with hemlock, red spruce and white pine.

In the spring, lush green valleys blossomed with wild crabapple trees, azaleas and rhododendrons, and in autumn, the fields were covered with the glow of asters, black-eyed Susans and goldenrod. White-tailed deer and black bears lived in the mountains with foxes, possums, minks and raccoons and the clean mountain streams were filled with bass, trout and walleyed pike.

But in the early fifties, newspaper and television people were calling this area "the land that time forgot."

To be sure, my Mingo County ancestors had contempt for law and order, and their bloody coal wars and family feuds earned the county the unenviable nickname of "Bloody" Mingo.

In 1934, Circuit Judge B. F. Howard, in appealing for an orderly election in the county seat of Williamson, referred to the county as the "Hell Hole of Creation."

Now, in 1988, as I reminisced, Judge Howard's stinging remarks still hinted at credibility.

I was born in 1937 and by the time I was seven I looked forward to watching opposing political factions battle it out on Election Day, sometimes shooting out their differences. Election day was the social event of the season in Mingo County, far surpassing the Fourth of July and Christmas rolled together.

My great-grandfather Ellison Hatfield, brother of Devil Anse, was killed on an election day in August 1882 across the river in Kentucky near Matewan.

Ellison was napping under a big apple tree near the polling place on Blackberry Creek just across the river from Matewan. As he awoke from his nap, brought on by too much moonshine, he strode up to the polling place wearing his straw hat, which had an extraordinary wide brim.

The hat attracted the attention of the crowd gathered around the polls and Ellison, relishing the attention, took off the hat and waved to the crowd.

Tolbert McCoy, the thirty-one year old son of Randolph McCoy, leader of the McCoy Clan, practically ran toward Ellison. As he reached Ellison, he screamed in his face, "I'm hell on earth."

Ellison looked up at him but didn't speak.

Again, full of liquor and jealous of the attention Ellison was receiving, McCoy screamed, "I'm hell on earth."

"You're a damn shit hog," replied Ellison.

McCoy struck at Ellison with a knife and left a large gash in his shoulder. Blood spurted over Ellison's shirt as the two fell to the ground.

Immediately, McCoy's two brothers, Homer and young Randolph, jumped in to help and before the group was separated my great grandfather was stabbed twenty-six times and shot once in the back.

As Ellison lay near death, Devil Anse and a posse of Hatfields slipped into Kentucky under cover of darkness and captured the three McCoy brothers.

Devil sent word to Randolph McCoy, leader of the McCoy clan, that if Ellison died he would kill the three McCoys. Ellison died at nightfall that same day and Devil and his band, which included my other great grandfather Moses Chafin, took the three McCoy brothers down on the banks of the Tug River at Matewan and shot them in the head. There they left the bodies for the McCoys to find the next morning.

With Ellison's murder and the subsequent murder of the McCoy brothers, the bloody feud intensified throughout Southern West Virginia and Eastern Kentucky.

Soon after this, Devil Anse's first wife died and he married Aunt Levicy Chafin, a sister of my great grandfather Moses. This made my dad, Tom, a double cousin to all the Hatfields, a fact which he noted at least ten thousand times during my childhood and ten thousand times during each of his political campaigns. Being double cousins to the Hatfields may not have been popular in Pike County, Kentucky, but it was good in Mingo because Tom held elective office for thirty consecutive years before retiring in 1980.

—⁓⁓⁓⁓—

Tom was called "Black" Tom to distinguish him from other Tom Chafins in the area. As soon as I was old enough to understand, I would beg him to tell me about the feud.

I especially enjoyed stories about the fabled romance between Johnse Hatfield, son of Devil Anse, and Roseanna McCoy, daughter of Randolph McCoy.

Tom, as a boy of nine or ten, had often visited and stayed for days at Devil's house. His vivid recall of the feud details made his stories dance with excitement.

"Tom," I would plead, "tell me about Johnse and Roseanna."

"Well," he would say, "it started like this. It was on Election Day in the spring of 1880 over on Blackberry Creek. As the day wore on, everybody noticed that Johnse and Roseanna had disappeared.

Johnse was a handsome lad, tall and slim with a neatly trimmed mustache. Unlike his seven brothers, he wore fancy clothes and was pleasant and mild-mannered and could talk his way out of anything.

Roseanna, who was said to be the prettiest girl in Pike County, had come to the election grounds with her brother Tolbert. She was a beautiful, black-haired girl and the pride of her father, Randolph.

Just as the sun was going down, Johnse and Roseanna finally returned to the election grounds. Her brother was already gone, and she became very frightened.

She was afraid to go home and after some tears and regret at having lost her virginity to a Hatfield on the riverbank in broad daylight, she convinced Johnse to take her home with him.

Devil Anse raised holy cane and refused to let Johnse marry her. Finally, the couple slipped away at night to Logan County where Johnse enjoyed full marital privileges without the shackles of matrimony.

Randolph McCoy, heartbroken, but still full of love for his daughter, kept sending Roseanna's sisters to persuade her to return home. About a year later, she left Johnse and went home.

The young couple tried many times to get back together, but Roseanna's brothers had strict orders to keep close guard on her.

Finally, she slipped away to her Aunt Betty McCoy's house on the banks of the Tug River near Stringtown. Johnse, of course, slipped across the river at night and the young couple continued their lovemaking.

One dark, hot night in August, the McCoys surrounded Betty McCoy's house and lay in wait. As Johnse stepped out of the water on the Kentucky side, he was greeted with a rifle to the head and captured. The McCoys planned to take him to Pikeville and surrender him to the Pike County authorities who wanted him on several charges.

Roseanna slipped away in the night and rode to Devil Anse's house and told Devil what had happened. Devil quickly rounded up a posse and intercepted the McCoys on their way to Pikeville. They brought Johnse back without any bloodshed.

Johnse and Roseanna never shared another kiss, but Johnse must have took a real likin' to McCoy women because he later married Roseanna's cousin, Nancy McCoy, and became so henpecked that Devil got fightin' mad.

Johnse and Roseanna was one of my favorite stories, almost as good as the Matewan Massacre and Smilin' Sid Hatfield.

In a few weeks, I would ask Tom to tell it again. He would and it would be even better because he would remember a new detail or two.

—◦◦◦◦◦◦—

One of my favorite tales was the "cow story." Soon after Tom quit the coal mines and opened a small grocery, he bought a real good milk cow. This cow was real good to give, he said.

This meant the cow gave lots of milk on a regular basis. Perhaps a gallon a day or whatever it is that a good cow gives.

One day Tom couldn't find his cow. He looked everywhere for the cow, but it was nowhere to be found. He sent my first cousin Dan Kinder up in Paps Branch to look for the cow, but Dan came back about an hour later all hot and sweaty and said, "Tom, that damn cow's not up in Paps Branch. Somebody has stoled that damn cow." In exasperation, Tom finally asked Pap (Pap was Allen, Tom's father) if he had seen his cow.

"Yep," said Pap, "I sold that cow to Old Man John Simpkins up at the head of the creek. He really needed a good cow."

"You sold my cow?"

"Yep."

"What did you get for her?" asked Tom.

"Well, I got a fair price," said Pap, brushing the question aside as if it were irrelevant.

Several days later, old man Simpkins came into Tom's grocery store. "Hi there John," said Tom. "I hear you bought yourself a cow."

"Yep," said the old man. "Me and Brother Allen traded a little."

"Is she a good one? Does she give good?"

"Best I ever seen," the old man replied.

"What did you have to give Pap for her?"

Without hesitation, old man Simpkins said, "I gave a fair price."

Through the years, I would occasionally ask Tom about the cow so I could hear the entire story again. I'm sure he knew that Pap gave his cow to the old man and that the two had collaborated on the sale price. He thought it was funny and enjoyed telling the story as much as I enjoyed hearing it.

—∿∿∿∿—

The Appalachian Region stretched from the rocky, plunging beauty of New York's Watkins Glen to the piney woodlands and foothills of Mississippi's Tombigbee and Alabama's Black Warrior Rivers. Years later, legislators would define its boundaries to embrace 297 counties in thirteen states and the entire state of West Virginia.

The peaks and valleys of the land were born of cataclysmic eruptions, intense heat, violent pressures from within the earth's interior and giant foldings of land masses that left the maze of high cross ridges.

As ages passed, ice and water slowly, relentlessly sculpted and eroded pinnacles and gorges, sawtooth ranges and winding valleys, creating a landscape at once forbidding and inviting, alternately fierce and yielding in its beauty, limited and prodigal in its resources.

During the 1600's, the land was settled largely by the Germans and Scotch-Irish. They were hungry for land, jealous of freedom, and ever ready to fight and strong in initiative.

They came early, endured and shaped the attitudes, products, legends, and realities that became the way of life in Appalachia. They had to "make do or do without," and they did both.

Matewan and Mingo County were smack dab in the middle of what the United States Congress would later call the Appalachian Region, and what author Harry Caudill would describe as an area of "social and political blight without parallel in the nation."

When the westward movement began years earlier, my ancestors remained in the narrow Appalachian valleys, choosing the isolation of the lush, green mountains where they could live according to their own rules.

Game was abundant and small hillside patches of tillable land provided ample sustenance. More importantly, here, they weren't answerable to any government that could effectively curtail their pursuit of happiness, or hemmed in by too many people.

While the Great War raged in Europe, life in Matewan in the 1940's was uncomplicated and pleasant. The marvel of a microwave baked potato was far in the future, and even an ignorant hillbilly knew that man would never walk on the moon.

Tom was sure we had reached the pinnacle of science and technology when he could turn on the radio and listen to the Grand Old Opry in faraway Nashville, Tennessee.

"What could possibly remain to be discovered?" he asked.

Little could he have imagined that by the time I was his age talk about microchip implants in a person's hand allowing one to trade and sell would be commonplace. He would have called it the mark of the beast and I'm not sure he wouldn't have been right.

—〜〜〜〜—

Life was easy. We were unaware of being poor or that the rest of the nation regarded us as underprivileged children of ignorant, hillbilly coal miners.

We had pork 'n' beans, bologna, and all the surplus US government commodity cheese we could eat. We had so much surplus commodity flour we used it to line the basepaths on our softball field. We didn't know about champagne and caviar and wouldn't have liked it anyway.

We climbed the mountains, dammed up the creek in summer, skated on the frozen ponds in winter, played softball on a field we made in the summer's dry creek bed, and dealt stud poker under the backyard cherry tree when we could come up with a few pennies.

When on occasion things slowed down, a daring game filled with courage and high adventure could be easily devised. One such game occurred in the summer of 1944 when I was seven.

My friends and I decided to meet behind the school house, take off all our clothes and run around the school building naked, screaming as loud as we could.

Participating in this adventure were first cousin Bo, Bennie Horn who we nicknamed Hornie, and his brother Tater Bug and Little Beaver Hardesty.

We were a scrawny, raggedy bunch of kids living up a dead-end hollow with nothing better to do on a long, hot summer afternoon. It seemed to me to be a brilliant idea. Just the thing to wake up the sleepy little community and put a little spice in the evening supper table conversation.

The school was just across the creek and faced the community and the backside of Tom's small grocery store. From their front porches, most of the townspeople had a full view of the front of the school. The backside of the school faced a steep hill and provided the privacy we needed to meet and take off our clothes.

I was the first to circle the school, naked and screaming. I knew nobody would be watching the first run and didn't start screaming until I was almost around the far corner. This would bring everyone out to see what was going on, and the next runner would have a big crowd of spectators.

The second run belonged to Bo. He edged slowly toward the corner and peeked around. His bare ass, perched on top of two skinny legs, was white as a sheet, contrasting sharply with the rest of his tanned body.

Tater Bug and Little Beaver kept saying, "go...go" until finally Bo looked back, spit a stream of tobacco juice, and fled around the corner.

I doubled over with laughter. By now a crowd of spectators would be gathered on the other side of the creek to watch the big show.

The crowd had indeed gathered and they whooped and yelled as Bo circled the school screaming like a wild Indian.

Finally he sped around the far corner, his daring mission accomplished.

The next runner was Hornie. He was the youngest and meanest of the gang and at the weight of fifty-five pounds was dangerous when he picked up a rock.

Aunt Sarah, Bo's mother, had said on several occasions that Hornie needed to be cleaned out with a dose of castor oil about once a week.

Hornie dashed around the corner immediately, not about to be outdone by me and Bo. About two-thirds of the way around the school, he suddenly stopped and ran back the other way.

When we were able to stop laughing, I asked him why he had come back. Panting and just about exhausted, he said, "There's too many people watching."

Tater Bug and Little Beaver chickened out and the adventure ended.

The townspeople no doubt appreciated the break from the boredom of the day as much as we did. Life was hard for them, and even a moment's distraction could turn a boring, uneventful day into one that would provide supper-table conversation for many days.

What Judge Howard called the "hellhole of creation," was to us the garden spot of the universe. We knew nothing else and assumed that everyone everywhere lived just as we did.

—*~~~~~*—

But, it was a wounded land. Wounded by neglect of its environment, the wanton rape of its natural resources and the absence of creative political leadership, the population inevitably became hopelessly mired in an endless cavern of apathy.

The tall, proud, green mountains, which had for centuries reached majestically toward the sky, had now become scarred and mutilated by thousands of coal company bulldozers.

Dreams of what might be tomorrow remained only in the minds of the very young who had not yet fully tasted the bitter flavor of economic and environmental degradation. But the dreams would die a little each year as the drudgery of surviving in the coalfields became reality.

Dreams had a way of dying early in Appalachia. A few years in the coalmines made young men old, quickly stealing any youthful ambitions remaining in their thoughts.

In the first grade, I mastered the alphabet and multiplication tables easily and was promoted from the first to the third grade. My best friends and cousins were in the third, and I was sure that school would now be more fun.

Two events happened the summer after third grade which I would always remember.

My most memorable experience during the summer following third grade was Ms. Bea's week-long summer Bible camp. Ms. Bea was a roving Bible teacher who periodically visited all the elementary schools.

During each visit she presented a Bible story with characters of felt she stuck on an easel. After the Bible story she played an accordian which was almost as big as she.

She was a wonderful woman and a good Christian but, for reasons all his own, God had placed her in the ugly group.

The day we arrived at camp was exciting. I had never been away from home for a whole week and the thought of getting away from Brother Don was reason enough to go.

Groups of eight kids were assigned to cabins with four sets of bunk beds. Upon entering my cabin I quickly threw my suitcase on a top bunk. It would be better for me, if the top collapsed, to fall down on someone rather than have someone fall down on me.

The nightly revival meetings were high-pressure sessions designed to get us all saved. Like many of the other youngsters I submitted and declared myself saved on the third night. Ms. Bea told me I would have to testify the following night.

The next night came soon and I was no sooner seated that Ms. Bea called on me. I stood without hesitation and said, "I'm saved in the blood of Jesus Christ and I don't care who knows it." I quickly sat down amid a rash of "amens" and "praise Gods."

Everyone seemed to be pleased, but I felt a little queasy since I didn't feel any different than I had when I was unsaved.

Finally the week ended and upon arriving home I didn't mention to anyone that I was saved. I guess that was good because the next day I had a mad-dog cussin' fight with Hornie. I lost the fight badly.

I later realized that I was trying to please Ms. Bea with my declaration of being saved. I felt like God would understand and wouldn't be too mad at me until I could really be saved someday.

But, I couldn't be saved right then. Not until I killed that damn Hornie with a baseball bat.

The other memorable event during the summer was when two older cousins, John Hatfield and Junebug Simpkins invited three of my gang, Bo, Hornie and me, to camp out with them. We were very excited as we gathered our provisions: a pot of pinto beans, cornbread, and fresh green onions, uncleaned but freshly pulled from Aunt Nannie's backyard garden.

Our campsite was only about three hundred yards from my house and just across a small creek from Bo's, under three tall sycamore trees at the base of the Hatfield Cemetery.

Our parents could practically see us from their front porches, but I imagined our brave troop as jungle explorers, roughing it with only marginal provisions to sustain life.

The only reason I remember the night was because of John and Junebug's gas fight. A gas fight was when everyone got under two large army blankets and covered their heads. The last one out was champion.

Being under two blankets with six boys who have just eaten numerous bowls of pinto beans is an experience few people ever have. I will never forget the awful, stinking odor.

I stayed under the blankets about three minutes and was about to die when I burst out gasping for air.

Bo was the next out and came out cussing a blue streak. "Them son-uh-bitches have shit all over everything," he gasped.

I shook with laughter as Hornie came bursting out from under the blankets, describing the terrible agony he had endured.

Finally, only John and Junebug were under the blankets. Every few minutes one of them would let off a loud fart, which seemed to cut right through the blankets.

Whenever one farted, they both crackled with laughter. Then, we started laughing and soon they would fart again. I couldn't understand how they stayed under the blankets.

As the laughter from the gas fight began to fade and the night grew deeper, the Hatfield Cemetery loomed ominous and, I reasoned if the dead could still vote they might also decide to pay us a visit. I told myself I wasn't scared, picked up my blanket and headed home.

At four o'clock in the morning, full of pinto beans and gas, I had had enough and staggered slowly upstairs to the clean, fresh smelling sheets in my upstairs bedroom.

Fifteen years later during a military police tear gas training session at Fort Gordon, Georgia, I remembered the gas war on that summer night in 1945. The gas under the blankets was worse than anything the army had to offer.

If the Army could have bottled that gas we could have wiped out the entire Nazi military machine in a matter of weeks.

Three

NINETEEN HUNDRED FORTY-FIVE was a significant year in my life. On July 10 my youngest brother Harry Truman Chafin, was born and six days later the first atomic bomb tested successfully at Alamogordo, New Mexico.

On August the sixth, the bomb was dropped on Hiroshima, virtually wiping out the Japanese city. Eight days later, Japan surrendered unconditionally and Emperor Hirohito announced defeat to his people.

The phrase "Kilroy was here" appeared almost overnight throughout the world wherever American GI's set foot. President Roosevelt died in office, and Eddie Arcaro, aboard Hoop Jr., won his third Kentucky Derby.

These events were completely overshadowed however, when Cousin Bo became the owner of a brand new shiny Daisy BB rifle.

I followed Bo around the neighborhood for two days begging to shoot the gun.

"I can't," he kept saying, "Mommy said if I let anybody play with the gun she'll take it away from me and lock it up in the attic."

Bo, like his father Leander, was hard to convince of anything. He lived next door and like Uncle Leander, was tall and thin and bullheaded. Uncle Leander was called "Black Lee" to distinguish him from other Chafins named Leander. I could never understand why there were three Chafins named Leander in the short span of six miles.

We had just moved into our new four-bedroom house and were delighted to have an indoor toilet. During my first eight years of life, I had been obliged to use an outhouse, which was across the road from our old house just above Tom's store.

If you had to go in a hurry, you not only risked messing your pants, but also the possibility of being run over by a coal truck. Once, when I had to go in a hurry, I couldn't get across the road. A car was coming one way, a truck the other, and I couldn't hold it. After the way was clear it was too late, and I walked stiff-legged to the outhouse and threw my underwear down the toilet.

I stuck with Bo until he ran out of BBs and then he became more conciliatory. I promised to come up with some BBs if he would let me shoot half of them. He agreed, and I hit upon a plan to get the ammunition.

It was a daring plan. Bo, Hornie and I would hitch a ride to Matewan and buy some BBs at the hardware store and hitch a ride back before anyone knew we were gone.

Early next morning, we slipped down the road about a quarter mile and began hitching a ride. We had learned how to hitch by watching our older cousins. All you had to do was stick out your thumb and wiggle it whenever a car came by.

In ten minutes or so an old man in a red pick-up truck stopped and we climbed into the back. Unfortunately, he only took us about four miles to the small, coal-mining community of Red Jacket.

Red Jacket was owned by the Red Jacket Coal Company. All the houses were the same one-story design and all were painted bright yellow. I always thought it strange that all the houses were painted the same color.

The once beautiful, seven-mile drive from New Town to Matewan, and a thousand other once beautiful drives in Central Appalachia, were fast becoming smoldering avenues of gob.

Gob, the refuse of rock and shale left over after coal was mined and processed and shipped away, was growing into mountains of refuse lining the highways and filling up the mountain hollows. Once tall, green mountains were being re-placed by tall, black mountains of gob.

The gob contained in the residue of coal often caught on fire and burned for years, leaving a lingering, foul-smelling odor and polluting the air with a sulfurous pall of haze and smoke. I smelled that odor for the first seventeen years of my life.

The big company store was also bright yellow and pow-dered with a thin black layer of coal dust. Tom told me that the miners charged their groceries there and on payday would find themselves with no pay due and deeper in debt. I was glad he had a store and we didn't have to charge groceries there.

I was apprehensive about walking through Red Jacket. I had heard that several mean boys lived in the community, and I suggested we stay where we were and hitch from there.

"No sense walking through Red Jacket," I said. "There might be some mad dogs loose that would get after us."

We hitched for about twenty minutes, but nobody would pick us up. Each driver who passed pointed his fingers as if he were going just down the road, but we didn't believe it and called each of them all the dirty names in our vocabulary.

"Who's that coming there?" asked Bo, his voice uncer-tain.

About three hundred yards up the road, three Red Jacket boys who seemed to be much bigger than we were walking toward us.

"Aw, that's just three old boys," I said, reassuring myself, but I was sure they would whip us good and began praying somebody would pick us up.

An old, blue pick-up truck was coming, and I began to pray harder. "Oh Lord," I prayed, "let it stop and pick us up and I'll never cuss again or steal any of Tom's cigarettes."

The old, blue truck stopped, and we happily jumped in back. As the truck pulled safely away Bo looked over at Hornie and asked, "Who was them son-of-a-bitches?"

"I don't know," replied Hornie, "but I guess we woulda had to whip their asses."

"Yeah," Bo agreed, "probably lucky for them we caught a ride."

The truck didn't stop until we got all the way to Matewan. I was excited. I had never been to Matewan by myself before. None of us had. I just hoped we wouldn't run into any bad McCoys while we were there.

The Matewan Massacre

Years earlier on May 19, 1920, my ancestors had participated in the county's most brutal wholesale killings on the town's main street by gunning down several Baldwin-Felts detectives who were in town evicting striking coal miners from company-owned houses. The Matewan Massacre was one of my favorite stories and every now and then I would ask Tom to tell it. He would.

He always began his stories with, "Well it started like this."

"'Two-gun' Smilin' Sid Hatfield, the police chief at Matewan and Mayor Cable Testerman supported the union the coal miners were trying to organize. What the mayor didn't know was that Sid was courting his beautiful young wife on the sly. Unaware of this romance, the mayor supported Sid and helped him get the police chief's job.

"When the miners started making progress organizing the union and went on strike, the Red Jacket Coal Company devised a plan to evict all the miners on strike from their company-owned houses."

I would occasionally interrupt to ask a question. "Who were Sid's parents?"

Matewan Train Depot Replica constructed by Massey Energy Company. Site of the Matewan Massacre. (Author's collection.)

"Well, now Sid wasn't really a full blooded Hatfield," he would say. "Sid's mother was the wife of Jake Hatfield, but his father was said to be a young man named Crabtree. Anyway, Sid was half Hatfield and most people would say that was plenty enough Hatfield to be in anybody."

The coal company got eviction notices for the striking miners and took the notices to the Baldwin-Felts Detective Agency in Bluefield.

On the evening of May 19, 1920, when Tom was nine years old, twelve Baldwin-Felts detectives boarded the train at Bluefield on their way to Matewan.

When they got to Matewan they went straight to the houses of striking miners and moved them out on the streets. The miners didn't put up any fight so the detectives went back to Matewan and waited quietly on the train to go back to Bluefield.

"Why didn't the miners resist?" I asked.

"Well, I think they might have known that Smilin' Sid had a surprise for 'em, but even if they didn't there wasn't much they could do. If you had two or three little children who were crying as they moved your furniture out on the road, you knew that if you resisted and started a fight those little children might get hurt. The smart thing to do was to do nothing.

"Anyway, it was a calm, warm spring evening and the town seemed real quiet and peaceful. The detectives cased their rifles and waited for the train.

"Smilin' Sid passed by Albert Felts, a brother of Tom Felts, one of the owners of the detective agency and nodded to him. Felts nodded back. As soon as they passed Smilin' Sid drew both pistols and shot Felts dead in the back of the head.

"Then, all hell broke loose. Shots rang out from the upstairs windows and a raging gun battle lasted for fifteen minutes. When the gunfire finally quieted seven detectives, Mayor Testerman and two striking miners lay dead in the street."

"How come Mayor Testerman got killed?" I asked.

"Well, now some say that in all the confusion Sid shot him in the head. I don't know if that's true or not, but seven days after they buried the mayor, Sid and the mayor's beautiful young widow were married.

"After the gun battle Sid and the striking miners danced in the streets until late at night. It was the biggest party ever held in Matewan."

"What happened to 'em?" I asked.

"Well, Sid and twenty-two others were indicted for the murder of the seven detectives. Their trial lasted nine weeks and when it ended every man on the jury voted not guilty."

Years later William G. Baldwin, head of the Baldwin-Felts Detective Agency slipped into the mountains to arrest one of the Hatfields on a moonshining charge and approached Devil Anse's house just as it was getting dark. Devil was known for his hospitality and often hosted travelers as well as family with the utmost kindness.

Baldwin asked Devil for lodging, being careful to conceal his identity.

"We ain't got much fancy but you're welcome to spend the night if you want," replied Devil.

Before daylight the next morning Baldwin heard someone approaching his bed and grabbed his gun.

"Mr. Baldwin if you'll hurry downstairs we got breakfast ready. You need to eat and get out of here 'cause if my boys find out you're here they'll kill you for sure."

Baldwin ate a hasty breakfast and Devil accompanied him a short way down the ridge. As they parted Mr. Baldwin said, "Mr. Hatfield, thank you for your hospitality and there's something I'd like to know."

"What's that, friend?" asked Devil.

"How did you know who I was?"

"Well, now have a safe trip to Bluefield," replied Devil and turned back up the ridge without a further word.

"Whatever happened to Smilin' Sid?" I asked.

"Well, the Baldwin-Felts people tricked him into coming to McDowell County to stand trial on some trumped-up charges.

"He went to Welch with Ed Chambers, a friend who lived there in Matewan, and they took their wives with them.

"When they walked up the court house steps in Welch, three Baldwin-Felts people shot them to death."

"What happened to the Baldwin people that killed them?"

"They had a big trial but they were all found not guilty."

I loved that story, but knew he wouldn't tell it to me again for at least two months. It would be better next time. There would be a few more details. I wanted to hear more about Mayor Testerman's beautiful young wife. Where did she come from? Was she a Hatfield or maybe a McCoy?

I couldn't wait two months. I wanted to know about the mayor's wife and I asked, "Where did the mayor's wife come from?"

"Well now, there's two or three stories about that," he said.

Oh Lord this is going to be good, I thought, hoping he would tell me all of them.

"Well, now one story is that she came off of Feds Creek, Kentucky, and had been tried by a grand jury for shooting her first husband. But, I don't believe that was true because Ernest Mounts a constable from Merrimac and a good friend of mine that you can trust told me there was no truth to that."

"What did Ernest say?" I asked.

"Well, now Ernest said that when Labella first got off the train at Matewan his first cousin Arbutus Maynard was the first one to talk with her. Arbutus worked at the Knotty Pine Restaurant and Labella came in and ordered a cup of coffee and an order of French fries."

"That's a strange name, Labella," I said.

"So Arbutus started talking with her and soon found out that she had bought a ticket in New Orleans for as far as she could go and the ticket just happened to end in Matewan, West Virginia."

"Do you think that's true?" I asked.

"Well, now Arbutus could be counted on for one thing and that was to tell the truth."

"So why did she leave New Orleans?" I asked. "Did she tell Arbutus?"

"Well, she did and she didn't. It seems like before she finished her French fries she had told Arbutus two different stories."

"Do you know what they were?" I asked eagerly.

"Well first she told her that she had been on a gamblin' riverboat and that her fiancé had been shot when another gambler accused him of dealing off the bottom and shot him dead."

"What was the second story?" I asked, trying not to sound too eager.

"Well, by the time she had finished her fries Arbutus knew that she didn't have five cents to her name. In fact, Arbutus gave her the French fries and coffee and tore up the check.

"That Arbutus was a good woman. She'd give you the shirt off her back."

"What did she do?" I asked. "No money. No place to go."

"Arbutus called Cabel Testerman and the mayor was at the Knotty Pine Restaurant in three minutes and ten seconds.

"According to Arbutus, lightning struck the mayor when he walked in the door and saw Labella.

"Labella spent the night at the mayor's apartment with the mayor and his mother. A week later the mayor and Labella were married.

"Unfortunately, the mayor wasn't the only official in town who recognized real beauty. Smilin' Sid, upon meeting the new bride, was also struck with a thunderbolt."

But all was peaceful in Matewan this day as we walked into the Matewan hardware store and hesitantly asked the sales clerk if he had any BBs.

The BBs were in the back of the store on the top shelf, and we followed the clerk, a heavy, mean-looking, red-faced man, and watched as he climbed up a ladder which slid from side to side on a rail attached to the top of the shelf.

He looked at me and asked how many I wanted.

"A dime's worth," I replied

He poured out the BBs in a brown paper bag and before we could say anything, he shot back up the ladder and placed the BB box on the top shelf.

Back down, he looked at Hornie and asked if he wanted anything.

"I wanted a dime's worth too," said Hornie.

The old man's face turned even redder, but back up the ladder he went. I looked at Hornie and bit my tongue to keep from laughing.

He poured out another dime's worth, gave them to Hornie and looked at Bo and asked, "Do you want a dime's worth too?"

"No," said Bo, "I don't have but..."

Before Bo could finish the clerk shot back up the ladder and placed the BBs on the top shelf. Back down the ladder he came, huffing and puffing, seemingly surprised that we were still there.

"What else, boys?" he asked, as if he wanted to be rid of us.

Bo said, "I wanted a nickel's worth of BBs."

"Get the hell out of here," he screamed, "and don't let me catch you smart-ass boys in here again."

We quickly departed trying to hold our laughter until we were safe outside. Twenty cents worth of BBs would have to last us forever because I was never going back.

In a few days, we were out of BBs and would have to wait until Thursday before we had cash again. Thursday was the day the junk man came to buy our scrap metal. He paid ten cents a pound for copper, four cents for iron and two cents for tin.

We were doing our part for the war effort by scrounging scrap metal and at the same time keeping ourselves a little spending money. In a good week, I could make up to a dollar. A bottle of pop was only a nickel and a dollar would go a long way. It would buy several rounds of RC Cola and Moon Pies.

One hot, summer day when Bo and Hornie and everyone was gone, I decided to go up into Paps Branch to search for scrap metal. Paps Branch was a hollow just below my house and extended about a mile up into the mountain.

At the top of the hollow, coal miners entered the portal in buggies powered by an electric motor. An insulated wooden pole attached to an overhead electric wire provided the power for the motor.

Coal was king in Paps Branch, Mingo County and West Virginia. Black Tom had quit the coal mines just after I was born. Rather than be switched from the day to night shift, he picked up his black dinner bucket, walked down the hollow and hung it up with no apparent prospects for providing my daily bread.

Soon thereafter, he borrowed $600 from his friend, Dan Chambers, at the Matewan National Bank on his signature and opened a small grocery store and ran for constable of Magnolia District. His successful candidacy began a string of thirty-seven consecutive years of serving in elective offices, ranging from constable to high sheriff of the county.

I knew that we weren't poor because Tom always seemed to have money. Not as much as I imagined, I'm sure, but every day during my three years in high school there was always fifty cents on the mantle for my lunch. I could buy a hot lunch at school for twenty-five cents and have a quarter for myself for whatever I wanted.

Instead, I opted to walk downtown with my friends for a leisurely lunch at the Smokehouse Grill. Hot dogs were twenty cents and a bottle of pop was ten cents. This left twenty cents for two games of pool. By the time I was a junior in high school, I, along with several friends, had become fairly adept with the cue.

If I had saved the extra twenty cents I could have faced each Saturday morning with a dollar which would have guaranteed an exciting Saturday.

With the coming of the Industrial Revolution in the late 1800's, coal became the fuel that fired the furnaces of the nation. But because the industry was so sensitive to fluctuations in the national economy, Mingo County, labeled the "Heart of the Billion Dollar Coal Field," quickly developed into a "boom or bust" area.

When oil flooded the American marketplace in the 1950's displacing coal as the nation's primary source of energy, Mingo County and all of Appalachia found itself faced with the prospect of prolonged economic "bust."

Absentee coal barons, of course, were totally unconcerned about the plight of the miners.

Some seventeen years later, the Appalachian Regional Development Act of 1965 would state,

> *The Congress of the United States hereby finds and declares that the Appalachian Region of the United States, while abundant in natural resources and rich in potential, lags behind the rest of the Nation in its economic growth and that its people have not shared properly in the Nation's prosperity...*

But insulated by our youth, we played happily and care-free in the mountains, unaware that we were poor and unconcerned that the rest of the nation considered us "Yesterday's People," and our land as the "Land that God Forgot."

Upon reaching the mine site at the top of Paps Branch, I stood on a hillside overlooking the rail tracks. The electric power wire was about fifteen feet below me on the opposite side of the tracks.

I had to take a leak so I decided to let it fly down on the rails. I held my pecker as high as I could and unwittingly tried to spray the electric wire overhanging the tracks.

Fortunately, my stream was too weak and I was spared from severe injury or electrocution. Memory of the near miss would later bring a cold sweat to my forehead.

I found a piece of rusted rail, which weighed about twenty pounds. I made sure none of the miners were in sight and put it on my shoulder and lit out down the mountain. It would bring seventy or eighty cents from the junk man, a good day's work.

Four

NINETEEN HUNDRED FORTY-SIX was an important year. Alabama beat Southern Cal 34-14 In the Rose Bowl. The Nobel Prize in Physiology or Medicine was awarded to Hermann Muller of Indiana University for his discovery of the production on mutations by X-ray irradiation, Ben Hogan won the PGA Golf Tournament and wage price controls were ended except for rent, sugar and rice.

All this was easily overshadowed by my newfound knowledge of sex, which an older cousin explained in living Mingo County Technicolor.

We were hangin' out in Asa Tate's Texaco Station, our favorite evening gathering place, next door to Tom's store, when, after our usual discussion of religion and local politics, the topic of how babies were made came up.

I couldn't believe babies were made that way. No way.

It sounded incredible. Why in the world would a man want to put his pecker in a woman and how did he do it. Not yet experienced in erections, I couldn't understand how that soft little thing could be put in anything except underwear.

It sounded downright nasty to me and I was sure my parents would never do such a horrible thing. I thought my cousin must be trying to pull a fast one on me.

But, as time will do, the years went by and as I began to have an occasional erection, the idea grew more plausible. I reasoned the erections must be for something and my cousin's explanation seemed better than anything else I could thing of.

It was not until the seventh grade in 1949, however, that I would experience my first sexual encounter.

Our next-door neighbor had opened a theater next door to our house in a large, gray cinder block building which had been an automobile garage and which still had large oily spots on the cement floor.

I was ecstatic to have such easy access to Roy Rogers, Gene Autry, and Gabby Hayes and I could always come up with a quarter whenever the picture changed.

My sexual debut occurred one Saturday afternoon during a double header starring Johnny Mack Brown and Lash LaRue.

I was sitting beside a seventh grade girl from Meador with whom I had had a sporadic flirtation. After two boxes of popcorn and a Hershey bar, she reached over and put her hand in mine. I started to jerk my hand away, but suddenly realized it felt good.

In a few minutes my hand began to sweat and I moved it to wipe it dry on my pants. Suddenly she began to rub my leg and I just sat there quietly as if it were the normal thing for her to do.

With each stroke she seemed to be getting higher and higher and my forehead began to sweat. My left leg was asleep and I wanted to move it something awful, but I was afraid if I moved she would stop.

I wasn't exactly sure what was happening and I felt just a little embarrassed, but I wasn't exactly predisposed to get up and find another seat. I might have moved if the building had been on fire.

I don't suppose you could, in today's liberated sexual climate, describe what I experienced as an educated male orgasm. But it towered over my previously best sensual experience of rubbing between my toes when I had poison ivy.

As Johnny Mack Brown rode off into the sunset, I scrambled out of the theater, not quite sure whether I had discovered something new and marvelous or whether I had peed all over myself.

This first sexual experience, although surprising and pleasant, was somewhat discomforting, but not enough so to doom me to a life of celibacy.

I graduated from the sixth grade in May 1948 and looked forward to attending Red Jacket Junior High School. I was eleven years old and becoming a little more aware of the difficulties of life in the coal-mining mountains of Mingo County.

While I attended junior high school, more than 445,000 people left West Virginia to look for work. Many of my relatives settled in Detroit, Columbus, Cincinnati and other urban centers.

Limited employment opportunities, low skills and little education restricted them to low-paying and insecure jobs in the city. They became lost in the maze of people, buildings and traffic. The same lack of education and training that held them down in the mountains shaped their lives in the city as well.

On holidays the roads were filled with automobiles with Ohio and Michigan license tags. We marveled at the big, shiny cars driven by our relatives who worked in the car plants in Cincinnati, Cleveland and Detroit.

But always, they yearned for home and the once beautiful, green mountains of Mingo County and hundreds of other places in Appalachia, although sadly their yearning could only be satisfied on long weekends and holidays.

As I completed the sixth grade, deep splits within the national Democratic Party and apparent public desire for a change, portended a national Republican victory.

Each evening, after supper, Tom sat in his favorite chair and between steady streams of Red Man tobacco amber, artfully splashed into the fireplace, warned me never to vote for a Republican.

I really didn't know why Tom and his friends didn't like Republicans. The ones I knew looked like ordinary people. None of them had horns or tails that I'd ever noticed.

When a Mr. Abraham from Williamson ran for a seat on the Mingo County Board of Education, Tom told me he couldn't win because he was a Jew.

"What's wrong with a Jew?" I asked. "Wasn't Jesus a Jew?"

"Oh, I like him," he said, "but people won't vote for a Jew."

"Well which one is worse?" I asked, "a Jew or a Republican?"

"You know the answer to that, don't you," he asked.

"No, I don't, which one?"

"A Republican is ten times worse than a Jew," he replied.

"Do you know any Republicans who are Jews? I asked.

"No, all the Jews I know are Democrats."

I wanted to ask him if he knew any black Jewish Republicans, but was afraid it would strain his heart. Such a mixture would be considered science fiction.

I was sure he was not oblivious to the fact that many people felt the Democratically-controlled Mingo County courthouse was the nation's leading bastion of political corruption and incompetency.

Always extremely interested in Tom's political observations, I was thoroughly brainwashed by the age of six and was actually nine or ten years old before I could admit to myself that a Republican could go to heaven.

Mingo County Democrats, who proudly called themselves "Hoover Democrats," consistently remembered the hard times of the Great Depression and outnumbered Mingo County Republicans by more than five to one, a ratio still intact in 1991.

Although they battled ferociously among themselves in the May primaries, they consistently healed their wounds and voted the straight Democratic ticket in the fall general elections.

They believed, like Black Tom, that the sorriest Democrat was better that the best Republican, and voted accordingly.

Being a Republican in Mingo County was an anomaly and I believed, as Tom said, that the expected victory of Thomas E. Dewey would bring swift and certain destruction to the country. I resigned myself to going without lunch in the seventh grade.

Thomas E. Dewey lost and I had lunch in the seventh grade. But when the coal industry appeared to bottom out in the early 1950's, central Appalachia and Mingo County were hit hard because of their unique dependence on mining. Being the rugged, hard-to-reach part of the region, central Appalachia had never been able to build economic diversity.

As oil flooded the marketplace, it appeared to sound the death knell for coal and, in doing so, doom southern West Virginia to a permanent economic depression from which it would never recover.

As economic horror stories became common in the early 1950's, I was primarily concerned with making the Red Jacket Junior High School basketball team.

As a puny one-hundred-five-pound seventh grader, I was quickly relegated to the second team where I would languish for three successive years. But, as always, I imagined myself as a sure-fire star who could, if given the chance, lead the Indians to greatness.

Moving up from constable, Black Tom was elected justice of the peace. In addition, he drove the school bus and still managed the small grocery at New Town.

The school bus was a constant source of aggravation because on mornings I wanted to skip school, Tom would stop in front of the house and blow the horn until I came out.

He repeated the process all along his ten-mile route and was often late in arriving at school, much to the ire of school principals.

I was beginning to realize that life was hard for many of my cousins and friends and began to notice they often came to school without lunch money and very little breakfast. Although the school provided lunch for those whose parents could not afford to pay, many would skip the meal rather than have their friends know they couldn't pay.

In the seventh grade, I learned there were three kinds of girls – pretty girls, ugly girls, and beyond ugly girls. Melody Hines was a small frail, blondish girl from Pigeon Creek who sat behind me in seventh grade history. Melody was at the bottom of the beyond ugly group. Her face would make a freight train take a dirt road.

She wore the funniest looking outfits I had ever seen. One day she wore a blue silk skirt, which looked like a party dress, a brown sweatshirt, a wide purple belt and a worn-out pair of tennis shoes with laces tied in knots. She looked comical.

When I passed her in the hall between History and English, I said, "You're looking mighty sharp today Melody."

She turned toward the locker alongside the wall and didn't respond. I hesitated a moment until she turned and was startled to see tears streaming down her cheeks. She turned and shut the locker and walked away without saying anything.

Before the ball game that evening, I told Jack McGill, my first cousin about it. Jack, a bright and handsome lad, could always explain a math problem whenever any of us were stumped. We got along remarkably well and often found ourselves with similar thoughts and on many occasions would start to say the same thing simultaneously.

Jack told me Melody's father had been killed in the mines about three weeks earlier. She had four sisters and two brothers, all living at home with their invalid mother.

I was so sorry I had commented about Melody's clothes. I was trying to be cute and had hurt her deeply. I hadn't meant to be cruel. When I went to bed that night I cried and prayed that God would take care of Melody and her family.

I made a special effort to be nice to her the rest of the year and by spring, and after persistent effort, she would smile and say hello when we passed in the hallway. I grew to like Melody and felt bad that she was in the beyond-ugly group.

Five

ON JANUARY 22, 1950, *The New York Times* announced that because of increasing costs in all phases of its newspaper operations, the newsstand price of the *Times* on weekdays in New York would be five cents.

In February President Truman invoked the Taft-Hartley Act in the coal strike, but only 30,000 of 400,000 miners stayed on the job in the bituminous coal fields. Local union leaders in Pennsylvania and West Virginia asserted that their men did not intend to go back to work without a contract, even if John L. Lewis ordered them to do so.

As these events were occurring I attained teenager status at thirteen. My most fervent wish was to be sixteen. Lots of things were possible at sixteen, but hardly anything was possible at thirteen. You couldn't drive so you couldn't have a real date. You had to be accompanied by a parent or an older cousin everywhere you went. You might as well be ten as thirteen.

It is possible, however to have fun at thirteen if you have twenty-seven cousins who are thirteen.

On the first day after school let out for the summer, I along with Bo, Hornie and Johnny Varney decided to build a dam on Mate Creek and have the biggest swimming hole in New Town.

The fact that raw sewage from all the houses in the community flowed directly into Mate Creek was little deterrent. We were determined to build the best swimming hole that had ever been built on Mate Creek.

We selected a site just back of Tom's store. The creek narrowed and two high banks on each side made it a perfect place for the dam.

We needed one large log about twenty feet long and about forty wooden planks to construct the dam. Plenty of sod and mud was available to plug between the planks. It would be one helluva dam and when full the water would be at least ten feet deep. This would give us enough depth for diving off the banks. Also, a big sycamore tree on the left side of the bank had a large limb about fifteen feet above the water. From the limb we could jump and create a tremendous splash.

After a week of hard work we put in the last plank and quickly dabbed sods of grass and mud in all the holes. The water rose slowly and after two days was about three feet deep.

"It's gonna take forever to fill," said Hornie.

"Not if we stop up the damn leaks," replied Johnny.

We dove into the project. Bo and I dug more sod and threw it down to Johnny who worked furiously to stop all the leaks.

The next morning the water had risen to five feet. Our spirits were buoyed. In a few more days the water would be deep enough for diving.

Each morning we gathered at the pool with three empty lard buckets and skimmed off the green, slimy stuff that gathered at the dam.

I suppose in the back of our minds we knew it was sewage and worse, but the thrill of the successful dam overrode any bacterial concerns we had.

After seven days the pool was two-thirds to the top of the dam. Johnny boldly announced he was going to jump from the Sycamore limb.

I said, "Johnny, you'll hit the bottom and break your legs because the water's not deep enough."

"Yeah, hell yes it's deep enough," he said, and up the tree he went.

Johnny lived with his mom about a mile east of New Town. His dad had been killed in the coalmines when he was six years old. He was a likable guy but he always had to be first.

Being an only child his mother insisted that he be home by dark every night. And he was obedient and usually left the gas station where we all hung out in time to walk the mile home before dark.

Johnny was the only boy in our gang that wasn't a cousin. His dad had moved to New Town from Pigeon Creek after getting a job at Number Seventeen Mine.

Despite our warnings that the pool wasn't deep enough to dive from the sycamore tree, Johnny insisted.

He stood up on the limb and crouched his knees as if ready to dive.

"Don't do it Johnny," yelled Bo, "you'll break your neck."

Just as he appeared ready to dive, his foot slipped and his head hit the sycamore limb making a crunching sound. He appeared to be lifeless as he hit the water.

We jumped in and pulled him out immediately but he was unconscious.

"Is he breathing?" asked Hornie.

I dashed to the store sure that he was dead.

"Tom, Tom, come and help us. Johnny fell from the Sycamore tree and I think he's dead."

Tom dashed out of the store with me on his heels and we were at the pool in a matter of seconds.

Johnny was white and lifeless as Tom knelt over him. He put his ear on Johnny's chest and told me to run and call the rescue squad at Matewan.

I ran home as fast as I could, found the telephone book and turned to the "R's." No rescue squad was listed.

"Hazel," I screamed, "come here and find the rescue squad number. Johnny Varney fell in the pool and is unconscious, maybe dead."

She found the number and called.

"They're coming," she said.

I dashed out the front door toward the pool and fell down the front porch steps and cut my leg on the concrete. It was bleeding bad but it wasn't important.

Surely Johnny wasn't dead, I thought. Nobody dies at thirteen.

I took a short cut between Tom's store and Uncle Pete's house. I could see the pool quicker that way. As I sped through Pete's back yard I saw Johnny sitting up and alive.

Nothing much else happened during the summer when I was thirteen. Except for Adele Maybell's annual Fourth of July visit.

The purpose of life according to Adele was to make love. Adele lived in Columbus, Ohio, and came to New Town every Fourth of July with her parents.

Her mother had moved to Columbus just after high school and married an Ohio boy but always yearned for the mountains and visited her sister faithfully every Fourth of July.

I first met Adele on July 4, 1948 and like my cousins always looked forward to Adele's arrival.

Adele seemed old for her age and by her own accounts had had numerous sexual affairs prior to her fourteenth birthday.

The Fourth of July was obviously our favorite holiday because Adele always provided exceptional entertainment. On the third of July, my four cousins drew straws to determine the order for sharing Adele's treasures. Hornie was lucky in the summer of 1950 and pulled the longest straw. Hornie liked to use big words and had a good vocabulary but often used the wrong word and after pulling the winning straw declared the little kleptomaniac Adele was his. Bo looked over at me and winked and I burst out laughing.

"What's so damn funny?" demanded Hornie.

"She's not a kleptomaniac you idiot, she's a nymphomaniac," answered Bo.

"Klepto, nympho, what the hell's the difference," Hornie replied.

Mr. and Mrs. Maybell always seemed pleased that we were all so glad to see Adele. Adele wasn't a bad looking girl. She was rather short and compact and her butt made a good impression on the back of her skirt.

For some reason Adele and I became friends and she seemed too sisterly for a sexual liaison with me. My cousins were glad I didn't pull a straw because it increased their holiday joy time.

In the summer of '50 Adele explained her philosophy of life to me. She was sure that making love was the primary purpose of life.

"People work in the coal mines, cook supper, mow the lawn and all the things they do to fill up the time until its time to make love," she said.

It seemed that her sexual activity with my cousins was the most natural thing in the world to Adele. She seemed to feel no remorse and in fact seemed happy all the time. Perhaps making a conquest of my poor, hillbilly cousins, gave her a sense of power, but they were quite willing to be conquered by Adele.

Adele was our kind of girl. She loved Jesus and America, had a liberal attitude about sex, was the queen of multiple orgasms and when old enough would undoubtedly vote a straight Democratic ticket. What more could be asked of a girl?

When the annual vacation ended the Maybells always stopped at Tom's store to say goodbye. My cousins and I were always there to bid the Maybells goodbye and safe journey to Columbus.

Adele always sparkled as she hugged us all goodbye. My cousins hoped she would retain her philosophy of life for another year.

She was the ultimate liberal and would, I was sure, grow up to be a Democratic Superstar in Ohio.

Six

IN THE SPRING OF 1951, the first commercial color TV broadcast was presented by the Columbia Broadcasting System. General Douglas MacArthur was relieved of all commands by President Truman. The Rochester Royals beat the New York Knickerbockers 79 to 75 for the NBA Basketball Championship, and I graduated from Red Jacket Junior High.

The three years at Red Jacket had gone by fast and I looked forward, with some apprehension, to attending Matewan High School. My friends would be going too, and we would still be riding Tom's bus, which always provided an extra measure of security.

This security blanket, however, had not protected me from my junior high school nemesis, Biff Johnson. On the first day of school in the seventh grade, Biff, upon entering geography class announced that I was in his seat. Although seats were not assigned, I sheepishly vacated my spot and moved to another seat. It was a mistake I would pay for, for the next two years.

Biff, according to his bully friends, was going to be a professional boxer. He had already attained heavyweight status in the seventh grade and looked to me to weigh at least two hundred pounds.

Unfortunately, I had a special place in Biff's heart. He bullied me at every opportunity and my hope that he would tire of bullying me and select another target never bore fruit.

In the eighth grade he started calling me "cutie" in front of my friends. I was embarrassed, but too scared to challenge Biff. If I started a fight with him, he would surely kill me. He had a seventy-five pound weight advantage and no doubt had been practicing his boxing. I wanted to tell Tom, but I was afraid he would think I was a coward which would be far worse that Biff's harassment.

The taunts continued through the seventh and eighth grades and on the first day of school in the ninth, began again, when Biff in front of my friends in gym class, announced that Tom was a crook.

Tom, a candidate for election to justice of the peace, had campaigned all summer for the November election. Lots of people called local politicians crooks, but Biff had made it personal for me. It was better to be whipped good by Biff than let this ultimate insult go unchallenged.

We had divided into two basketball teams and as we gathered around the circle for jump ball, I calmly walked over to Biff, smiled and hit him in the face with my fist as hard as I could.

He didn't fall but apparently was so stunned he didn't immediately strike back. I hit him again and blood gushed from his nose. I knew I was dead and for a split second wanted to run from the gym.

Instead of running I hit him again and again until he grabbed me with both arms and we fell to the floor, rolling and grunting and cursing.

He was so strong I couldn't get loose. He was squeezing me to death and I couldn't breathe. The blood from his nose was running onto my face. Unable to breathe and about to pass out, I managed to raise my head just enough to bite his ear with all the strength left in my teeth.

He let loose and jumped up screaming, "you've bit off my ear, you've bit off my ear."

He was holding his nose with one hand and his ear with the other and his entire face was covered with blood. It looked like I had won the battle but I didn't fell victorious.

Surely he will now kill me, I thought, but there was nothing I could do but run. It was a thought I most seriously considered.

At that moment the loud, wonderful shrill of the physical education teacher's whistle gave me a reprieve. Biff would have to kill me another day.

The next morning Biff and I were called to Principal Varney's office. I arrived first and the secretary told me to have a seat. Biff came in a few minutes later and sat opposite me. We looked at each other and I was glad when he looked away first.

He had a band-aid on his left ear but otherwise looked fine. There were no signs that the blood all over his face had left any damage.

The principal was a friend of my dad's and I was determined to tell him the truth. He asked me first, "What happened Andrew?"

"Well, sir, Biff has been bullying me for two years and yesterday in gym class he called my dad a crook and that was all I could take."

"Did you do that, Biff?" he asked.

"Yes, sir. I was just kidding," replied Biff.

"Have you boys got this problem solved or do I have to solve it?" he asked.

I said, "Yes sir, it's solved as far as I'm concerned."

"What about you, Biff?" asked Mr. Varney.

"Yes sir," answered Biff.

"Yes sir what?"

"Yes sir, it's solved."

"Good," replied Mr. Varney, "you boys get to class and I'm warning you both I'd better not hear of any more problems between you."

As it often is with bullies, Biff never bothered me again. I think he thought I was crazy. I feared a lawsuit but it never came. What judge or jury would believe that such a wimp as I could hurt a big stud like Biff?

As I entered the tenth grade free of the shackles of terror, social scientists were beginning to talk and write about the plight of Appalachia, commenting that one in three families lived below the poverty level with per capita income more than one-third below the national level.

It would take fourteen years, however, for the President's Appalachian Regional Commission to report:

Graphs and tables can hardly relate the acutely personal story of a child in the remote valley, his horizon of opportunity limited to the enclosing hills; nor the despair of his father who, idled by forces beyond his control and seeing no prospects of future employment, must live month in and month out with the vision of that child repeating his own history.

Such personal despair during the 1950s caused two million people to leave Appalachia. More of my friends and relatives left for urban centers to find work, often moving in with and causing hardship to those who had gone before.

Those leaving were mostly younger people with marketable skills thus exacerbating the shortage of skilled manpower in the region. But, unable to find jobs at home, the only avenue remaining led directly to Columbus, Cincinnati, Detroit or other urban areas where many moved into "hillbilly ghettos."

Central Appalachia was hardest hit because its coal industry had to compete with cheap oil and natural gas, thus producing low wages, widespread unemployment and a lack of public funds to modernize its infrastructure.

Although rich in natural resources, Mingo and all of Appalachia lacked the means to exploit the vast supplies of coal and timber.

We had sold our land and mineral rights for pennies an acre, unaware that the coal underneath was worth thousands of dollars an acre. We had become not the entrepreneurs, but the laborers whose heritage was mountains of gob and red dog.

Helplessly we watched the wealth produced by coal and timber find its home in faraway places. It floated downstream and rode out on rails in the coal cars to enrich non-resident owners who had bought rights to the land for a few cents per acre.

But, like thousands of other young Appalachians, I entered the tenth grade a fifteen-year-old, one-hundred twenty-five pound sophomore, not fully concerned about the plight of my people nor aware that instead of searching for the great American dream, they were searching for survival.

It would not be until nine years later in 1960 that national attention would be brought to Appalachia poverty, with John F. Kennedy's historic visit to West Virginia in quest of the 1960 Democratic presidential nomination.

Political observers regarded West Virginia as a "key" state in Kennedy's election strategy. While the purpose of his visit was to demonstrate the appeal of a Catholic to an almost entirely Protestant constituency, his visit yielded another unexpected result.

Kennedy was so moved by the poverty he found he pledged to launch a special program for Appalachia if elected President.

Although Mingo County Democrats would cast the majority of their votes for Hubert Humphrey, Kennedy carried the state substantially and regarded it a key in his successful first ballot victory at the Democratic National Convention in Los Angeles.

The seed had been planted and would, in 1965, result in President Lyndon B. Johnson signing into law the Appalachian Regional Development Act. This milestone legislation would launch a new experiment in government, a partnership between local, state and federal governments designed to help Appalachians lift themselves from economic and social obscurity.

Prior to the enactment of this most needed legislation, the associate editor of the Johnstown, Pennsylvania *Tribune-Democrat* said, "Appalachia is a figment of the bureaucrat imagination, designed to justify a vast new spending program of the federal government, and the employment of a host of new federal employees to invade the area and bring its people into the utopia of the New Frontier."

Some figment.

—◌◌◌◌◌◌—

Meanwhile, my greatest concern was to make the basketball team and proudly wear the green and white of the Matewan Tigers. Much to my dismay, I was again relegated to the second team where I would again languish for three years, my vision of stardom diminished to the hopes of seeing a few minutes of action in the "B" team game.

New friends came easily and by October I was in love with three girls, all at the same time. I was most in love with Helen, but she persistently failed to acknowledge my existence.

She was a small, exquisitely proportioned lass from North Matewan and had almost-blonde hair, green eyes, ruby-red lips and all that stuff that makes a teenage boy drool.

The system for letting a girl know you were interested was to have a friend tell her you were "stuck" on her and then have the friend report her reaction. If she responded negatively the friend was supposed to tell her he was only kidding, thus sparing you the embarrassment of rejection.

Being unable to convince Helen that I was alive, I dispatched Scotty Varney on a Cupid's mission. Everybody liked Scotty and he had a knack for making friends easily. Rather rotund and jolly, he could approach anyone with his quick smile and infectious laughter.

Scotty lived at Low Gap, a small community about four miles down the creek from New Town. He had been a true and trusted friend since the seventh grade at Red Jacket. He quickly agreed to approach Helen with the message. The plan would be implemented the next day between biology and journalism classes.

Scotty did his job, but the message he brought back was disastrous. Helen's reply to the fact that I was "stuck" on her was, "Who's he?"

That was a definite "no."

Young hearts mend fast and I got over Helen when she started dating a two-hundred pound football player from Pigeon Creek. Better to have loved and lost than have your eyes blackened by a strapping stud who outweighed you by eighty pounds.

I would be fifteen in January and still had another year to wait before I could drive. I was sure my efforts at romance would greatly increase if I could ever get old enough to get a driver's license.

As 1952 rang in, Mingo Countians began to prepare early for the spring election. The Korean War had diminished President Truman's prospects for re-election and he announced early that he would not be a candidate for a second term.

Although Mingo County Democrats would reject "I like Ike" buttons and would support Adlai Stevenson of Illinois, they would be on the losing end of a landslide.

Eisenhower lost big as expected in Mingo, but carried the nation with an overwhelming electoral margin. To the further distress of West Virginians, he led the Republican Party to victory in both houses of Congress, marking the first time since 1931 that the Republicans controlled both the executive and legislative branches of government at the same time.

Democrats spread the rumor that the statue of Chief Logan standing outside the Mingo County Courthouse wept real tears the morning after Eisenhower was elected.

Tom told me many old timers believed the rumor.

"Did he really weep?" I asked.

"No," he replied, "but a lot of us good old Democrats did."

"Why would he weep?" I asked. "Was he a Democrat?"

"I don't know," he laughed, "if he was a Democrat or not, but I hear he's been voting since 1932."

Chief Logan of the Mingo tribe. (Author's collection.)
Rumored to have always voted a straight Democratic ticket.

Black Tom and other faithful party regulars won their local elections easily, but lamented the national Republican victory and assured themselves the country would soon revert to the deep depression they had experienced under Herbert Hoover. "It would serve them right for voting for a Republican," Tom assured me.

Gloom settled over the already-depressed coalfields, and, as the 1953 national depression loomed closer, careless coal-mining practices continued to scar thousands of acres of hillsides and pollute thousands of miles of mountain streams. It seemed that unhappiness was compulsory in coal mining camps.

Uncontrolled burning of coal continued to pollute the air in the tight valley communities and the haphazard cutting of timber turned an ample rainfall into disastrous floods throughout the mountain empire.

Unconcerned about the consequences of the environmental disasters being reaped upon the land, I completed my sophomore year at Matewan High. I had my learner's permit and the occasional, if illegal, use of Tom's 1951 Chevrolet.

— ~~~~~ —

Hugh Jones O'Keefe was the classic Appalachian coal miner. Twenty years in the mines and the late stages of "black lung" made his voice erupt into deep, rasping coughs whenever he laughed or whenever his lungs required more than a normal amount of oxygen.

Years of crawling in low coal mine entries had bowed his back and lined his eyes with what seemed to be a thin, black, permanent ring of coal dust.

The white strings in the back of his blue overalls dangled untied down the seat of his pants, reaching halfway to his ankles.

Each evening after work, Hugh stopped by Tom's store to pick up grocery items his family needed and sliced bologna and cakes for packing the small, black lunch bucket he carried to work.

As a somewhat reluctant clerk in Tom's grocery, I knew all the regular customers. Like Hugh, many of them charged their groceries and paid their bills on payday.

I missed seeing Hugh for a day or two and asked Tom where he was.

"He's been laid off," Tom replied. "They've laid off a hundred miners at Number Seventeen Mine and I don't know how the poor man is going to make it."

"What about his bill?" I asked.

"Listen," he said. "Don't worry a thing about his bill. You let him have anything he wants. He's got three little children up there living in that tar paper shack and he's an honest man. You let him have anything he wants."

"What about his bill?" I repeated. "What if he can't pay his bill?"

Hugh came by the following day and handed me a grocery order written on a piece of brown paper bag. Bread, milk, lard, flour, Karo syrup, pinto beans and two pounds of sliced bologna were scribbled on the paper.

I filled the order, placed it on the counter in an empty pork and beans box and thanked him.

When Tom came in later that evening, I said, "Hugh was in today and charged about ten dollars worth of groceries."

"That's all right. You let him have anything he wants," he said.

"His bill is up to forty-five dollars and he didn't pay it Saturday. Saturday was payday, wasn't it?"

"Come back here Andy," he snapped. "I want to tell you something. Hugh has been trading with me for ten years and has paid his account in full every payday. He's a good man and he's got three little children to feed, and I don't care how high his bill gets or how long it takes for him to pay it, you give him anything he wants in this store."

"Okay, Okay," I said. "I'll give him the store if he wants it."

"Now just a minute, now you wait just a minute. Do you think it would be right to refuse him credit when he's laid off and got no way to feed his family? What kind of man would I be to do that?" he asked.

I knew he was right, and I knew he would give Hugh the last can of beans in the store. "Well, that's fine with me," I replied. "It's your store and I was just telling you what his bill was."

Hugh continued to come to the store every few days and his bill grew to well over four hundred dollars before he was called back to work at Number Seventeen.

Each payday, he would pay for the groceries he had charged the previous two weeks and pay ten or fifteen on his old bill.

In late summer, Hugh was killed in a mining accident. Twenty tons of rock had fallen on him at Number Seventeen Mine. He still owed two hundred forty dollars.

At Tom's insistence, I went with him to Hugh's burial service. I watched as they lowered his casket into the ground, and I didn't like looking at the high piles of dirt beside the hole in the ground. It didn't seem right to put a man down into a hole and throw dirt over him.

I wondered what his life's greatest joy had been. What had been the happiest day of his life, the happiest hour? What had his life meant? Would it have mattered if he had never been born? Maybe he had never had a happy day, I thought. What a sad, miserable way to live and how horrible to be put away in a hole in the ground on a little hill in Mingo County.

Nobody in London or New York knew Hugh had died or lived. Of all the people in the world, only a few in New Town knew Hugh had ever existed. He was born poor, lived poor and died poor without ever having experienced the sweet smell of success.

I hoped my life wouldn't be that way. I didn't want to be like the thousands of Hugh O'Keefes who lived and died without anyone ever knowing it. I wanted to hit a grand slam in the bottom of the ninth with my team down three runs.

Preacher Jim Meade conducted the graveside service. Hardly anyone was there except Tom and me and his wife and those three little kids.

"Let us pray," said Preacher Meade.

"Almighty God, we now return our brother Hugh to the ground, but we know his soul has gone to be with you in Heaven. Thank you Lord for our Savior Jesus Christ who has the keys to death…."

"Oh God, Oh God," cried Mrs. O'Keefe in a loud pitiful voice. "Oh God, Oh God, Oh God," she continued to wail as Preacher Meade continued to pray.

An old lady amongst the few mourners kept saying, "Help her Lord, help her Lord," and Preacher Meade kept praying.

I was really glad to walk down off the cemetery. I felt so sorry for Mrs. O'Keefe. I wondered if Hugh was really in Heaven.

On the way home, I asked Tom what he was going to do about Hugh's bill at the store.

"Hugh's accounts have all been settled," he said. "They've all been paid in full."

"Why did the Preacher say Hugh was in Heaven?" I asked. "Hugh never set foot inside a church house."

"You don't have to go to church to go to Heaven," he said. "Hugh was an honest man and God is a merciful God."

Everyone I knew who had died had gone to Heaven, even those who I had heard other people say were mean as hell.

As Tom pulled the car into the driveway at the store, he looked at me and asked, "Do you think we did right by letting Hugh charge those groceries when he was laid off last year?"

"Yes," I said. "I never really wanted to refuse him credit." I thought about the $240 Hugh still owed, but didn't say anything.

"I know you didn't," he said.

For the first time I realized that no matter how rich or famous a person was, death would always be the great equalizer.

—〰〰〰—

The summer was drawing to a close and each day I waited impatiently for the evening softball game. We gathered at the field, chose sides and battled until it was too dark to see the ball.

The third base side of our field was partially in the creek bed and was sprinkled with thousands of tiny rocks. The infield was level, but behind second base the field slanted sharply uphill toward the elementary school.

The elementary school outhouse was in short centerfield, standing conspicuously at the highest point of the field. The field slanted downhill from the outhouse back toward the school.

The centerfielder had to play toward left field in order to see the batter.

One evening during a particularly heated game, my team trailed by three runs in the bottom of the ninth. Disputed plays, followed by ten-minute cursing sessions, had already stopped the game three times and darkness was hurrying as Bo came to bat.

Bo lined a single to left. Little Beaver beat out a slow roller to third, and Tater Bug was safe at first when the first baseman failed to come up with a low throw.

After two pop-ups with the bases loaded, I came to bat determined to get a hit. I lofted a high, but short fly ball to centerfield, which landed squarely on top of the outhouse and took a crazy bounce toward left field. But the time the left fielder got the ball in, I had crossed home plate with the winning run.

As we shouted and cheered, Hornie, the opposing pitcher, began to claim that any ball hitting the outhouse on the fly was an automatic double.

"That's a good rule," Bo shouted. "But you can't make a rule after the game starts."

"It's been a rule all year," Hornie yelled.

"Well, I've never heard of it," said Bo.

"Well, I don't care if you've heard of it or not, you son-of-a-bitch, that's the rule," shouted Hornie.

"Shit on you," said Bo. "We've won the game."

"Shit on you and every Chafin alive," screamed Hornie.

"Double shit on you and all the Horns," countered Bo.

"Triple shit on you and all Chafins who ever lived," shouted Hornie.

To my amazement Bo countered with, "Quadruple shit on all Horns and Hatfields."

Hornie, unfamiliar with the word, but sensing some vile, filthy term had been attributed to his kinfolk, yelled, "If anybody's quadruple it's you damn Chafins."

Johnny Varney standing on first base and watching the argument in amusement began to laugh and then I started and soon both teams were laughing.

As we left the field and crossed the bridge to Tom's store for our evening ice-cold R.C. Cola, I put my arm around Hornie and whispered, "I hope you're on my team tomorrow."

Only a few of us knew what quadruple meant but it had eased the tension allowing us to part as friends until tomorrow's game when once again the overwhelming need to win would provoke the losing team to ridicule the winner's kinfolk.

Perhaps because we had so little, the need to win a meaningless softball game magnified itself into some sort of victory in our quest to attain recognition of our existence.

As I spent the long, hot afternoons working in the store, the summer dragged slowly by with only the evening ball games to break the monotony.

By late August, I had decided there were two things I was never going to do - work in the mines or run a grocery store.

When at last the summer faded, I was more than ready to begin my junior year at Matewan High, but still somewhat leery of Mrs. Montgomery's English class.

Gray and slightly bowed after many years of teaching, she still demanded obedience and attention, neither of which I and my associates appreciated.

In the tenth, Cousin Jack sat in front of me, Melvin Le-Master behind me, and Scotty to my left. Most teachers separated us, but not Mrs. Montgomery because she demanded full control of the class and had it.

"What is an anecdote?" she asked, looking around the classroom as if searching for someone who actually might know. I dropped my eyes toward the desk fearing that eye contact might prompt her to ask me.

"What is an anecdote, Scotty?" she repeated.

"An anecdote is a skin disease, something like acne," replied Scotty, as the class erupted with laughter.

Mrs. Montgomery pounded the desk with her ruler and the room quietened immediately.

"What is an anecdote, Melvin?" she asked.

"An anecdote is something like an antidote, you take it after swallowing poison."

Again the class erupted and again the ruler slammed down on the desk bringing silence.

I bit my tongue to keep from laughing. I didn't know what an anecdote was, but it was so funny I was about to burst trying not to laugh.

"Does anyone know the definition of an anecdote?" She asked.

Silence.

"Tomorrow," she said, "I want each of you to bring a written definition of an anecdote, and you Andrew, since you find ignorance so amusing, you be prepared to present an anecdote to the class."

After class, Jack, Scotty, and I headed for the library. As we crossed the cement lawn between the administration building and library, Scotty asked, "What the hell is an anecdote?"

Laughing, Jack said, "It's a skin disease, dammit. Look Andy, Scotty's got anecdotes all over his body."

"Damn, Scotty," I said. "He's right. There's little red anecdotes sticking out all over your face."

"You all kiss the little red anecdote on my black ass," he said, and we shook with laughter as we continued toward the library in our quest to define an anecdote.

Defining an anecdote proved to be a difficult task, but finally we decided it was merely a short, amusing, interesting story usually about a famous person.

I set about trying to find one that was amusing and interesting, which would put me back in the good graces of Mrs. Montgomery. I searched until lunchtime, but couldn't find one that satisfied me. I decided to continue looking later, but other classes and the evening softball game required my time.

The next morning seemed to come quickly and still I had no anecdote. Mrs. Montgomery would have a hissy. I had to come up with an anecdote by ten o'clock.

As she closed the classroom door she walked to her desk, picked up her ruler and looked directly at me.

"Andrew, come up and present your anecdote to the class," she said.

I was afraid to tell her I didn't have an anecdote, so I stood and walked to the front of the class just to the left of her desk. She sat there like a queen bee, tapping her ruler lightly on the desk.

I glanced at Jack and Scotty and they appeared to be struggling to keep from laughing. Scotty had his hands over his face, peeking at me through his fingers. I bit my lip. I dared not laugh.

Suddenly I blurted out:

> Humpty Dumpty sat on a wall
> Humpty Dumpty had a great fall
> All the King's horses and all the
> King's men couldn't put Humpty
> together again.

The class erupted into total pandemonium. Mrs. Montgomery jumped up and slammed her ruler against the desk, but the laughter grew even louder.

Again she pounded on the desk, and the ruler snapped in two pieces. Half of it flew out on the floor, and she continued to rap the desk with the other half. I thought I could feel the heat coming from her face. She looked as if she could spit out fire and brimstone. I was scared and tickled at the same time and didn't know whether to cry or laugh.

Tears were streaming down Melvin's cheeks. Scotty's arms were folded on his desk with his head buried down between them. The rest of his body was shaking as if he were having some kind of seizure.

Johnny Varney's head was laid back and he was laughing uncontrollably. Hammer Hatfield was hysterical. All semblance of order had vanished. For the first time in history, English 101 was out of control. Pandemonium reigned. Chaos was king. God, it was good.

I was expelled from school for two days. When I returned, I was greeted with special homework for two weeks, but I had earned the undying admiration of my classmates.

Mrs. Montgomery never seemed to like me after that.

Three weeks later she sent me to the library for talking in class. I had only asked Cousin Jack if he was going to play in our evening softball game, but her tolerance for me was at an all-time low.

My punishment was to give the class a five-minute presentation on U.S. Presidents. I liked to study the presidents and regarded the assignment more a reward than punishment.

During my study I discovered a Chafin had been a candidate for president in 1908 and 1912. Eugene W. Chafin running on the Prohibition ticket in 1908 garnered 252,821 votes coming in fourth in a seven-candidate race. He lost to the winner William H. Taft, William J. Bryan and Socialist candidate Eugene V. Debbs but outpolled Thomas L. Hisgen running on the Independence ticket, Thomas E. Watson of the Peoples ticket and August Gillhaus of the Socialist Labor Party.

This would make an excellent presentation for class, give me the opportunity to let my classmates know that a Chafin had run for president as well as give me a chance to trick Tom on a political history question.

I waited until the evening news was off before asking, "Tom, did you know that a Chafin once ran for president of the United States?" I was sure I had him stumped.

"Well, I believe he run twice, once in 1908 and then again in 1912," he replied.

I wondered how he could know that but moved on to the next question.

"What ticket did he run on and who was his vice presidential candidate?" I asked confidently.

"He ran on the Prohibition ticket and his running mate was Aaron S. Watkins."

"Holy cow," I said, "how did you know that? I've got one more question for you, what state was he from?"

I couldn't find the answer in the library and if the library didn't have it there was no way he would know. I waited and finally he looked at me and grinned and said, "Andy you need to study your history better. You should know that."

"Well, where then?" I asked, confident he didn't know.

"Eugene Chafin was from Wisconsin and he was a writer and lawyer. His running mate Watkins was from Ohio and was a lawyer and president of Ashbury College."

Mrs. Montgomery's 1954 Journalism class. I'm the one at the arrow.
(Photo courtesy of Hester Kinder Keatley and Shirley Harth Robertson)

"How do you know that Tom?" I asked. "You were one year old when Chafin run for president in 1912."

"I've got to get out to the store," he said and as he opened the door he turned and called, "Hazel, come in here and teach Andy some history."

"One more question," I yelled, "was Chafin any kin to us?"

"I don't know," he replied, "why don't you find that out for us?"

I got an "A" on my presentation to the class and Mrs. Montgomery seemed pleased. Several trips to the library were fruitless. I couldn't find anything on Eugene W. Chafin other than he was a presidential candidate in 1908 and 1912.

But since there aren't that many Chafins in the world I've always felt he is somewhere in my family tree.

Seven

DURING THE SUMMER OF 1952, the keel of the first atomic submarine, the *Nautilus*, was dedicated at Groton, Connecticut. The Republican National Convention nominated General Dwight D. Eisenhower for the presidency, and American stockholders numbered six and a half million, 76 percent of whom earned less than ten thousand dollars a year after taxes.

Such facts of history paled in comparison to a weird "peeping Tom" incident, which would be stamped in my mind forever.

Evangeline McCoy was a gorgeous, beautiful, dark-haired girl of nineteen who lived about a half mile up Mate Creek. She was a sophomore at Morris Harvey College in Charleston and coveted by all the young men in New Town, especially Cousin Hammer Hatfield, who approved of lustful, natural liaisons between consenting teenagers.

Hammer was the son of Fanny Mae Jones Hatfield, who was one of Tom's second or third cousins. Fanny Mae had been married briefly to a Hatfield, but the marriage had produced no children. Two years after her divorce she unexpectedly gave birth to Hammer. I never knew who Hammer's father was and I had asked Tom on several occasions who his father was, but he never gave me a definitive answer. I'm not sure he really knew.

Hammer looked a lot like the Hatfield boys who lived over at Beech Creek. They were all short, fast and good baseball players just like Hammer. But, it didn't matter because Hammer was one of my best friends.

I listened intently as Hammer outlined his devious plot to view the fair Vangie in the nude. I certainly wasn't morally above taking a peek at Vangie. But, the fear of getting caught in the cornfield, which reached up to her bathroom window, outweighed my desire to watch the fair maiden wash her well-shaped backside.

Old Man McCoy was rumored to have shot and killed a man in his younger days, and we all were afraid to pester him. We never stole his corn or pulled pranks on him at Halloween because we were afraid he might shoot at us.

Early in September, however, on a hot, balmy night seemingly made for consummation of romance, which, unfortunately, I had not yet tasted, my youthful lust overcame my better sense and I decided to implement Hammer's plan, without Hammer. One person would, of course, make less noise and have less chance of getting caught.

As darkness arrived, I sauntered up Mate Creek in what I hoped was an inconspicuous trod to the point where Vangie's cornfield joined the road.

Mate Creek was just a trickle of a stream in August. Its banks were lined with plastic Clorox bottles and other debris washed down from the last big rain. We dammed it up at narrow places and made swimming pools. It was probably loaded with every disease known to mankind, but none of us ever got sick.

I looked around. I looked up the road and down the road and stepped quietly into the cornfield. Vangie's house was about fifty yards from the road and I could see a light in her window.

I couldn't believe I was doing it, but, slowly, quietly, I made my way toward the house. Every few feet I would stop and squat and listen for any sounds. If anyone caught me, I was going to say I was walking down the road and suddenly nature called and I had to go. I didn't know what I would say if they asked why I had come so far into the cornfield to do it.

As I neared the house, I could see someone in the window. A little closer and I realized it was Vangie. "Great gobs of goose poop," I whispered. "It's her and she's naked as a jaybird."

The fair Vangie was taking a bath.

Before I could move closer, the unmistakable, terrifying snap of a cornstalk just to my right brought terror to my heart. I lit out through the cornfield as fast as I could with Old Man McCoy right behind me. I could hear him furiously tearing down his own cornstalks to catch me. It seemed like he might be gaining on me.

I knew if he had already killed a man he would surely kill me if he caught me, and I ran faster than I ever ran before. I made it through the corn and headed down the road as fast as I could go.

A car was coming in the distance, and I was afraid he might recognize me if the lights shined on me. I dashed off the road over the bank and slid into the creek up to my ass. "Oh, Lord," I thought, "I won't be able to run as fast with wet shoes."

I lay there, too tired to move. I was as limp as a wet noodle, but my heart pounded so hard it scared me, and I thought I might have a heart attack if McCoy didn't kill me first.

Tomorrow was the first day of school and I wondered what my friends would say if I were found dead in Mate Creek after a "peeping Tom" incident.

I visualized headlines in tomorrow's paper, "New Town Boy Killed After Peeping Tom Incident."

The car passed by, and I slowly eased up the creek bank to see if anyone was coming. I froze. Someone was coming and he was running. It had to be McCoy. I began to cry.

"Oh, Lord," I prayed, "if you don't let him catch me, I swear I'll never peep at another girl as long as I live. And I'll go to church Lord and I'll be good the rest of my life."

I crawled back down the bank and waited. I thanked God as hard as I could when running footsteps passed by.

I eased back up and watched the dark figure still running away from me. As the moon moved from behind the cloud, I recognized the running figure.

"Damn," I thought, "all that hard praying and it wasn't even Old Man McCoy. I cussed angrily as I watched Cousin Hammer slow his pace as he neared the lights of Tom's store.

On the school bus the next morning, I motioned for Hammer to sit beside me.

"How's it going?" I asked.

"Okay," he replied.

"What did you do last night?" I asked.

"Oh, I listened to the Reds and Dodgers game."

I looked at him and grinned and then leaned over and whispered, "You scared the shit out of me in Vangie's cornfield last night."

Startled, he turned and looked at me and we broke into uncontrollable laughter. It was an experience we would never forget or ever share with anyone else. At least not for thirty-four years and the 1988 class reunion.

After surviving the peeping Tom incident I decided to take Tom's often-given advice to "straighten up and fly right." After all, I was a junior in high school and despite my best efforts of resistance, I was becoming mature. I was fifteen and could be expected to be more responsible.

My efforts to act more mature and responsible lasted three days but ended abruptly on Friday night when Bo and Hornie came by.

"They're having a poker game up at Mackie's," said Bo, "Let's go up."

"Okay," I said, "let me get my jacket."

Mackie was my first cousin and lived about a half-mile from our house. He had been in the Army but was discharged after being shot in the foot. He had been awarded a Purple Heart and I always wondered why he hadn't been awarded a purple foot. He had been married twice but his second wife had left him and he now lived alone.

Mackie was the consummate New York Yankees fan. A walking encyclopedia of Yankee statistics, he worshipped Phil Rizzuto and Yogi Berra and any player who had ever worn a Yankee uniform.

Another first cousin, Dan Chafin, was also an avid Yankee fan. Dan and I usually hung out at Tom's grocery during the summer days because we had nothing to do but listen to the ball game. Mackie and Dan were such intense Yankee fans, they finally drove me to the point where my favorite team was any team that was playing the Yankees. I was really a closet Cincinnati Redlegs fan but the Reds were so bad I kept it from Mackie and Dan.

The poker game must have been going on since early afternoon. A case of Falls City beer which had apparently been consumed by the players, was empty except for one remaining bottle.

"Want a beer, Dock?" Mackie asked.

"Yeah," I said. My nickname was Andy Dock but I never knew where it came from. The only Dock I had ever heard of was a man named Dock Hatfield who lived over on Beech Creek, but he wasn't any kin to me.

Mackie reached down and plucked the last bottle and handed it to me.

"We need something to drink, Dock," said Mackie. "Why don't you and Bo and Hornie go up to Aunt Kizzie's and get us a pint of moonshine?"

"Yeah, sure," I said. "We'll go. Give us two dollars and your car keys."

Bo and Hornie piled in the car with me and we were off to Mitchell Branch to see Aunt Kizzie.

Kizzie was a little old black woman who according to rumor made the best moonshine in the county. She lived at the head of Mitchell Branch three miles from the Red Jacket Coal Company store.

I was apprehensive as we pulled up in front of Kizzie's house. I handed the two dollars to Bo and asked Hornie to go with him and get the moonshine.

"Tell her Mackie sent you," I said.

In a few minutes they came back and slid into the car.

"Did you get it?" I asked.

"Yeah, we got it," said Hornie.

I pulled away quickly and we headed back to New Town. As soon as we were safely out of Mitchell Branch I pulled off the road.

"Let's take a gander at it, " I said.

Hornie pulled it out of his back pocket and handed it to me. It was clear and white and looked like a pint of water.

"Do you want to taste it?" I asked.

"Yeah, let's taste it," said Bo.

I opened it and handed it to Hornie.

"Don't we need a chaser?" he asked.

"No," I replied. "We're he-men. We don't need a chaser."

Hornie turned it up and took a sip and made the awfulest looking face and handed it to Bo. Bo took a sip, tried to conceal the burning feeling that I was sure rushed down his throat and handed it to me.

I took a sip and felt a hot flash shoot down my throat and up through my nose. I thought for a second I might vomit but held my nose until it passed. I screwed the lid on, handed it to Hornie and pulled back on the road.

We stopped three more times on the four-mile stretch to New Town. By the time we got back to Mackie's we were singing, "What A Friend We Have In Jesus." We were all drunk and the moonshine was more than half gone.

I handed the car keys and the bottle to Mackie. He looked at it and then at us and said, "You damn boys are drunk."

We laughed. Everything seemed funny.

"We wanted to make sure it wasn't poisoned before we brought it back," said Hornie.

"Well, I'll tell you one damn thing," said Mackie, "if it's poison you damn boys are dead."

We laughed harder.

Although I would be around moonshine many times during my teenage years, I would never again taste the powerful potion. It was simply too awful. As Hornie said on the way back to Mackie's, it really did taste like horseshit.

Eight

IN THE SUMMER OF 1953, the Baseball Hall of Fame inducted Jay Houna Dean, universally known as "Dizzy" Dean, and outfielder Aloysius H. "Al" Simmons. Julius and Ethel Rosenburg were executed at Sing Sing Prison, the first civilians to be executed in the United States for espionage and Ben Hogan beat Sam Snead to win his fourth U.S. Open Golf Tournament, and I was glad it was summertime.

I was glad to pass English with a "D," and I looked forward to doing nothing – having no responsibility, being as free as a bird. I would have to work in the store and although it would be boring, it was a good lazy man's job.

When you're sixteen, you expect something exciting to happen each day. When it doesn't, you expect it the next day. When it doesn't happen the third day, you get bored and try to make it happen.

I rarely had to wait three days for something exciting to happen during the summer of '53, because adventures like the tent revival meeting up on Blackberry Creek kept jumping out at me.

Blackberry Creek was where my great grandfather Ellison had been murdered by the McCoy brothers, but it was peaceful now. All the Hatfields and McCoys had intermarried and one rarely heard of conflict between the two clans now.

We were going to the tent revival meeting because Josh Hatfield's girlfriend would be there. Josh had whined repeatedly all week long, "I gotta bound to see her."

Josh lived up past Meador and had been adopted by our gang after he defended Hornie when Hornie started a fight with a big boy from Red Jacket. The boy was about twice Hornie's size, but he never started a fight he could win and at the age of fourteen had had twenty-four fights and boasted a record of no wins and twenty-four losses. I lost two decisions myself after jumping in to help him, and then decided to just let him get whipped whenever he started a fight.

The old boy from Red Jacket beat up Hornie and Josh both, but the fact that Josh tried to help set well with us and we let him play on our softball team. He couldn't hit a lick and couldn't catch a ball in a wash tub but had a good attitude. He was quick to help us cuss out the other team during our frequent disagreements and would fight at the drop of a hat.

Josh was a lanky, skinny tenth grader with a semi-bad case of acne and the ugliest boy in our entire gang, maybe the whole county. I wondered how he ever got a girlfriend and decided she must be in the "beyond ugly" group, maybe even uglier than Josh.

They met when she came to Josh's aunt's house at Meador during another tent meeting back in the spring. Josh swore she was the prettiest girl on Blackberry Creek.

The lights from the big, grayish-brown revival tent glowed brightly in the dusk as we reached Blackberry. In a few minutes, it would be dark and the lights from the big tent would cast an eerie glow against the green mountains.

A big sign with white letters on the side of tent said, "Old Time Gospel Revival, Sinners Welcome." As we neared the tent Bo said, "I reckon we're welcome."

We peeped through the open flap and eased quietly inside. Folding chairs, some metal and some wood, were lined in neat little rows. Bare electric light bulbs dangled from low-hanging lines, reaching from one side of the tent to the other.

"Amen...Amen...," shouted the Preacher, "let's turn to page ninety-eight and sing all four verses of "Amazing Grace."

I had peeped in at church services many times at New Town but rarely went inside. Once, when I had, one of my older cousins went up front and got saved. She danced and spoke in strange tongues and I couldn't understand a word she said. It sounded crazy to me and scared me a little and I never went back inside after that.

Ever since I had gone to Hugh O'Keefe's funeral with Tom, I had been afraid of dying. Once when I was hiking up behind the Hatfield Cemetery, I grew tired and laid down on a smooth, grassy spot and stared at the gravestones. I wondered if I dug up the graves and opened the caskets what the bodies would look like.

As I lay there quietly, I pondered what life and death were all about. I wondered if I were any more important than a cow or an insect. A man is born, eats, sleeps, reproduces and dies, so that others can be born, eat, sleep, reproduce and die. The cycle never ends, I thought. What is the use of it all?

As I lay looking at the gravestones, the bright, sunny day suddenly turned dark and cloudy. I saw people walking up through the cemetery. They walked slowly as if they really weren't going anywhere. They were all dressed the same in gray, dusty-looking robes. I thought I could see dust fly when they moved. I wondered why I wasn't afraid.

My great-grandfather Ellison was in front, leading the others. Behind him was Devil Anse carrying an old rusted rifle. They came to the fence and stopped and looked at me. Somehow I knew they couldn't come past the fence enclosing the cemetery.

Ellison called my name, and I wondered how he recognized me. I could see holes in his robe and knew they were made by the stab wounds inflicted by the McCoys. His hair was long and dark and his eyes were like two pools of darkness and he seemed to be sad.

"Grandfather Ellison," I said. "What are your doing?"

"I've come for you my son," he said.

I began to cry. They wanted me to come and live with them, but they didn't seem to be in Heaven. "But, I have to go home." I said, "It's getting dark and Tom will come looking for me."

"No, my son, it's time for you to come with us," he said.

"But I'm too young to die. I'm only ten years old," I cried.

"Come, my son," he said, extending his hand to me.

I didn't want to touch him, but something made me reach for his hand. Just as I was about to touch him, his hand turned into bones and I jerked away. The people behind Ellison began to laugh. Their faces began to multiply until thousands of faces were staring at me and laughing wildly.

They're all ghosts, I thought, and they're trying to trick me into being one too. I must get away, I thought, and dashed down the hill as fast as I could go. When I got to the bottom I looked back up at the cemetery. They all had moved to the front fence and were looking down at me, still laughing.

"Why are you laughing?" I shouted. "You're not going to get me, I'm still alive." They began to laugh louder.

I looked up and the sky was blue again. The sun was back out and the cemetery was calm. "What a terrible dream," I said aloud as I jumped to my feet and ran down the hill.

I wondered what the dream had meant. Did it mean anything? Did it mean I was going to die soon? I glanced back toward the cemetery. It was quiet and peaceful in the summer sun.

When my cousin came to the store the next day, I asked her how it felt to be saved. Her reply was, "What's it to you, asshole? Gimme a loaf of bread." I guess she hadn't got a full dose of religion.

"Where's she at, Josh?" asked Bo.

"That's her up there in the third row beside that woman in that red dress," replied Josh.

"She's the ugliest bitch I ever seen in my life," said Bo.

When Josh got mad he turned a bright red and perhaps just a little uglier. He was bright red and ugly. I'm sure his parents never regarded him as the pick of the litter.

"You son-of-a-bitchin' bastard," he said. "Keep your damn mouth shut."

Bo looked at Josh and grinned, infuriating him more. Bo was a master at provoking the other kids to the very edge of their endurance before backing off. I just laughed when he got on my case and he would soon tire of bothering me.

"This world is not my home. I'm just a-passing through," boomed the preacher. "Are you saved tonight, brother? Are you washed in the blood of the Lamb? Don't leave this tent tonight, brother. Don't leave this tent tonight, sister. Little boy...little girl...don't leave this tent tonight without Jesus in your heart," he shouted.

I hoped he wouldn't start preaching on fire and brimstone and Hell because it scared me when they talked about going to Hell and never being able to get out. It seemed to me that there had to be an end to everything. I couldn't understand eternity.

"Everybody that's saved raise your hand," the preacher ordered and raised both his arms above his head.

Just about everybody raised their hands except me and Bo and Josh.

"Look," said Bo, "she's got her hands up, Josh. She's saved, Josh... no nookie for you, Josh," he kidded. "She's saved by the blood, boy," he repeated.

Josh was turning red again. "Come on outside, you prick," said Josh.

"Don't talk like that in church, boy," Bo reprimanded, suddenly becoming righteous.

"Well, keep your damn mouth shut then," said Josh

Bo let him cool off for a while and then started on him again. "Why don't she come back here and see you?" Bo asked.

"She can't get up and come now," said Josh

"Well, we can't stay over here all night," said Bo. "I'm ready to go."

"Well go on then and see who gives a damn."

"How will you get back to New Town?"

"I'll get back."

"I don't see why you wanted to come over here and see that ugly old girl for anyway," said Bo.

"She's not ugly, you asshole."

"She looks like a corn cob with hair on it," said Bo.

I remembered the matter didn't seem to be approaching resolution when suddenly Josh turned and hit Bo square in the face as hard as he could. It sounded like thunder. The preacher stopped and everybody turned around to look.

I moved over to the side and tried to act as if I were by myself. They rolled on the ground, grunting, kicking, gouging and cussing. I couldn't believe what I was seeing.

Some giant of a man in a pair of blue-bibbed overalls got both of them by the neck and it looked like their feet were off the ground as he dragged them outside. "You boys are headed for Hell fire," the man said. "You get away from here and don't ever come back. We're decent people, and we're trying to serve the Lord."

It took me twenty minutes to get them in the car. Bo got in the back seat, but Josh refused to get in. "Come on, Joshie," I begged. "You can ride in the front seat with me." Finally he got in and we headed home in Tom's 1952 Chevrolet.

No one said a word on the way back until we got to Red Jacket, three miles from home, when Bo said, "There's one thing I'd like to know, Josh."

Josh didn't reply.

"There's one thing I'd like to know, Josh," Bo repeated.

"What's that, asshole?" asked Josh.

"Have you ever had sex?"

"Damn right I've had sex."

"When?" asked Bo.

"Lots of times," replied Josh.

"When was the last time?" Bo asked.

"Last week," said Josh.

"Don't you wish you'd had somebody to share it with?"

Josh wasn't the brightest bulb in the lamp but when I burst out laughing he realized that he had been had again and demanded I, "Stop the damn car."

"But Josh, we're almost there," I said.

"Stop the damn car right now."

I pulled over and stopped and Josh yanked the door open and got out.

It was only two miles to New Town. I knew he could make it home so I pulled away.

Three days later Josh came into Tom's store and acted as if nothing had happened. We chatted amicably about nothing and I hoped Bo wouldn't come by.

I had been scared that God might punish me for my part in disrupting Church services. It had been Bo's fault and it was funny but I didn't know if God had a sense of humor.

Bo actually liked Josh. He just liked to provoke people and see how far he could push them, but had underestimated Josh's breaking point. Josh was a little crazy anyway. Everybody said his parents were too closely related to be married.

I remembered my eighth-grade history teacher telling us that Edgar Allen Poe and Charles Darwin had married their cousins and that Poe had married his cousin when she was thirteen. I didn't know how close kinship could be before it prohibited marriage but Josh's parents were apparently on the edge. Or over.

Intermarriage was necessitated by the region's isolation and cousin marriages were fairly common and necessary in the isolated hollows. I didn't know if that mattered, but Josh was a little funny.

I never saw Josh's girlfriend after that and he never mentioned her again. I never said anything to Josh but she was in the "beyond ugly" group. Anyway, the fight with Bo ended the budding romance.

—~~~~~—

There was one thing I liked about Josh and that was that he could be trusted. While Adele Mayhew made the Fourth of July our favorite holiday, Halloween was a close second.

The Halloween of 1953 almost became a terrible tragedy for Josh, Bo, Hornie, and me. Always eager to pull off the most outlandish prank, we had devised an exciting, devilish plot for the Halloween of 1953.

Old Man Beecher Mounts lived just a half-mile up Double Camp Hollow, about three miles from my house. He lived with his wife Maude who everybody called Sister Maudie. We had nothing against Beecher, but the fact was that his outhouse sat perilously close to the edge of the bank and could with a good push tumble over into Mate Creek.

Just after dark we parked our car in a dark cove and walked quietly up the dirt road toward Old Man Beecher's house. We were determined to push the outhouse into Mate Creek and run like hell to our waiting escape car.

Quietly and deftly we slipped toward the defenseless outhouse. Beecher's house was just across the road and there was danger that he might hear the sliding structure as it slid down the bank and burst out of his house with a shotgun.

I worried about that but it was too late now. I imagined that we were Hatfields about to spring a surprise night raid on the McCoys.

No one spoke as we slipped to the outhouse and simultaneously pushed. Over it went and away we went running furiously toward the car.

Once safe in the car we quickly sped down Mate Creek to the safety of Tom's store.

I arose about ten o'clock the day after Halloween and ambled out on the front porch. The sun was shining bright on a beautiful Indian summer day.

Next door Uncle Leander was wiping the windshield of his new Ford pickup truck. When he saw me he motioned for me to come over.

I looked at him, surprised that he wanted to say something to me, but walked down the steps and next door to his truck.

"Did you hear about Old Man Beecher Mounts?" he asked.

"No," I replied, "did he die or something?"

"Somebody pushed his outhouse into the creek last night," he said.

"What did they do that for?" I asked.

"Well, I figured it was some of you boys."

"I don't know anything about it," I lied. "I was down at Red Jacket with Bo and Josh and Hornie at a Halloween Party."

"It wouldn't have been so bad, but Old Man Beecher was in the outhouse when they pushed it over," he said. "He came out of that outhouse covered with shit all the way up to his neck and he is ready to kill whoever did it. I hope you and Bo weren't in on it."

"Where's Bo?" I asked.

"He's never got up yet, he's still in bed."

"Well, we didn't have nothing to do with it," I said and walked back to my house.

I sat on the front porch until Bo finally came out.

"Bo," I yelled, "come here."

"Did Uncle Leander tell you about Beecher Mounts?" I asked.

"No, he's gone to Matewan and I just got up."

"We've got to go talk with Hornie and Josh," I exclaimed. "Old Man Beecher was in that outhouse and he will kill us all if he finds out we did it."

When we found Josh and Hornie we formed a circle and held hands and swore never to tell or admit our deed to another living soul until Old Man Beecher died.

We all kept our word and never told. Beecher questioned folks for two years, but never found out who pushed his outhouse into Mate Creek.

—ᴧᴧᴧᴧᴧᴧ—

The tent meeting was less spectacular than the one we had attended on Pigeon Creek a few weeks earlier. The traveling evangelist was from Arkansas and his tent was much larger and fancier. All the folding chairs were white and arranged in perfect rows.

The stage was elevated two steps higher than the seats and was decorated with a large picture of Jesus, which was surrounded by flowers and two large lampposts.

The preacher was an enormous black-haired man who must have weighed four hundred pounds. His gray suit, which looked expensive, must have consumed twenty yards of material. It fitted him well.

We sat on the back row as usual. Bo and Hammer were with me. The tent was filled to capacity. I didn't see a single empty seat. It was the first time I had ever heard a faith healer. I'd heard that a woman with throat cancer had been healed the night before but I wasn't sure I believed in faith healing although I knew God could heal whomever he pleased. And, I didn't believe you had to have a preacher to be healed. If you had enough faith you could be healed without a middleman.

The music was simply great. The preacher and his wife, a blonde with large black eyebrows and weighing in at about 220, sang "Amazing Grace" and it made the hairs on the back of my neck stand up.

After three songs the preacher boomed, "I can't heal anybody, but Jesus can, Jesus can," about five times and some in the crowd started shouting, "Jesus can, Jesus can."

It didn't take long for the preacher to work the crowd into a frenzy.

"I feel the spirit flowing through my body," he shouted.

I thought that it would take a lot of spirit to fill his body, but discarded the thought immediately because I was afraid God might not be pleased with such a thought. I tried but I couldn't control my thoughts. Mean things were always slipping into my mind and I wondered if I might be possessed with an evil spirit.

Whenever I had bad thoughts I always remembered the dream I had when I was in the first grade. My bedroom was small and had a fireplace which was always burning in the winter. On the other side of the wall in the living room was another fireplace. They were back to back. They provided heat for the house. The coal stove in the kitchen also provided heat, but was mostly used for cooking.

I must have gone to sleep gazing at the fireplace. I was awakened by God's voice saying, "don't worry Andy, I'll watch over you."

In the fireplace I could see angels surrounded by beautiful colors which I later would recall looked like the NBC TV peacock.

When I awakened the following morning, the dream comforted me. I asked myself if it was a dream or had God really spoken to me.

From that morning whenever I got in trouble or was scared about something, I would remember the dream and tell myself not to worry because God had promised to watch over me.

"I feel the spirit," the preacher boomed again. "Can you feel it?" he shouted. "Can you feel it? Oh praise God, can you feel it?"

An elderly white-haired lady on the front row was holding her hands over her head and shouting, "Heal me Jesus, heal me Jesus."

Every time the preacher would pause to take a breath she would raise her hands and cry, "Heal me Jesus."

I didn't feel like the preacher was ready to heal anyone yet, and I think she was becoming a distraction.

He pointed his finger at her and then motioned for her to come up on the stage. "Amens" spread through the crowd as she hobbled to the stage.

The preacher reached for her hand and asked, "What's your name sister?"

"Beulah Jane Mitchell," she responded, and then repeated it, "I'm Beulah Jane Mitchell."

"What's your problem, Sister Beulah?" the preacher asked so loud I thought he must have wanted it to be heard in Heaven.

She said something to the preacher but I couldn't hear what she said.

"Our sister has arthritis in her back so bad she can't stand the pain," said the preacher.

"Do you believe God can heal you?" he asked.

I couldn't hear what she said but she was nodding her head yes.

Again he shouted, "Do you believe God can heal you?"

The crowd, sensing a miracle, suddenly became very quiet and he asked again, "Do you believe God can heal you, sister?"

He put his hands on her back and shouted, "Be healed in the name of Jesus. Be healed sister!"

Her arms went up and she began to dance around the stage showing no symptoms of arthritis or pain of any kind.

The crowd erupted into "Amens" and "Praise Gods," as she continued dancing around the stage.

After dancing for three minutes, Beulah Jane forgot about the two steps down from the stage. She missed the first step and went crashing to the ground underneath a white folding chair. As they carried her out, I heard someone say she had broken her leg in two places.

I wondered if her arthritis had really been healed. I sure hoped it had because at her age it would take a long time for her leg to heal. I was puzzled that God could heal arthritis but not a broken leg. I wondered why He didn't heal her leg and make it a grand slam.

The tent meeting was supposed to last through Sunday, but the preacher shut it down the next morning, three days early and left Pigeon Creek. I never went to hear another faith-healin' preacher. I had my peacock dream I could depend on and I wasn't sure I believed in faith healing. I would ask Tom about it tomorrow.

—◦◦◦◦◦◦—

The summer drifted slowly in the hot, little grocery store. Now that I was older, it was becoming harder to have fun. I couldn't run around the school house naked...couldn't hunt for scrap iron up Paps Branch...and didn't have the nerve to explore Old Man McCoy's cornfield again.

The coal miners stopped every evening after work and picked up their groceries. I enjoyed observing them, but felt bad that they had to work so hard in the mines and never seemed to get any better off.

Hugh O'Keefe's widow married a boy from Beech Creek who was a lot younger than she. He moved into the tarpaper shack with her and the three kids. Tom warned me to be careful about letting him charge groceries. He said he didn't have a job and wouldn't work if he had one.

I hoped he would be good to the children. I didn't like to see children mistreated. Sometimes I would give them free candy or ice cream, but it seemed like everybody was poor and the store would go broke if I gave away too much.

But, living from day to day, from payday to payday, had become the norm for Appalachian coal miners and their families. Avenues for improvement were permanently detoured and it seemed each day only compounded the gloom, misery and despair from which they would never escape.

Perhaps the most striking feature of American history in the 1950's was what many termed as the miracle of American economic expansion. Americans liked to believe that their growing prosperity was reaching every area of society, but they were wrong. Appalachia was experiencing an almost total economic collapse. Poor schools, inadequate health care, narrow, twisting roads and lack of job opportunities had left Mingo County and all of Appalachia almost entirely shut off from the mainstream of American life.

From the beginning, the mountains had imposed an economy of scarcity, and a hardy lifestyle nurtured independence and aversion to rules and regulations. Unfortunately, this had resulted in an economic and political structure that differed dramatically from the interdependent and prosperous society of the nation.

Independence and an inbred desire to "make your own rules" had been sufficient for survival in the past but this independence had quickly become obsolete and inadequate in coping with economic realities of modern life.

Thus, descendants of mountain people were faced with a struggle for survival, unable to cope with life in the 1950s with only a heritage of tillable hillside patches of land.

Coal company towns like Red Jacket that provided housing and other needs to miners, while freezing out more normal community development, were being abandoned by coal operators, leaving people without viable communities and job opportunities, trapped in a downward economic spiral.

I could feel the "trodden-down spirit," of the miners when they came into the store each evening. They were below the bottom, looking up to see the bottom, looking halfheartedly for anything that would sustain them and their families.

We were tied to the mountains by geography. We were born in a "fixed" place and were immobile because of faulty transportation, educational and political systems. Few of us would escape this geographical poverty simply because our parents did not realize the escape clause to poverty was education.

Hugh O'Keefe's story happened a million times to a million coal-mining Appalachians. It was heartbreaking, but it was a cold hard fact.

I had one more year of high school, and I vowed never to become one of them, hopelessly mired in circumstances beyond my control.

There's no way I could know that in the future my life's work would be devoted to improving the quality of life for these people. My hope was to someday be a journalist or writer of novels or some kind of great literary figure.

From time to time I would write and submit short story manuscripts which were always returned with rejection slips. My only sale would be to *Ladies Circle* magazine in May of 1969 when they would pay me seventy-five dollars for an article.

My article title would be on the magazine cover which was adorned with a beautiful photo of Jackie Kennedy. Being able to write something that someone would pay for was a thrill, but the pressures of work and family had to take precedence over my feeble literary efforts. Anyway, after reading that Margaret Mitchell's classic, *Gone With the Wind* was rejected by more that twenty-five publishers, I decided I'd best concentrate on my day job.

—◆◆◆◆◆◆—

One hot, boring July Saturday night the gang decided to have a cookout. The cookout would have one menu item – corn on the cob. Josh, Bo, Hornie and Hammer joined me in the planning. First, we would get a tub from Aunt Nannie's back porch and take it to our campsite, fill it with water and start a big fire under it. Then we would go up to uncle Kirk Hatfield's and raid his cornfield.

Uncle Kirk's field was on the opposite side of the road from his house and we went in the backside of his corn where it would be easy picking.

We were in my old 1949 Chevrolet when we eased over the back of the cornfield. We tried to be quiet, but the ears made a terrible snapping noise as we plucked them from the stalks.

We threw four-dozen "roastneers" in the car and slipped away in the darkness. We ate corn late into the night.

The next morning about 9:30 Tom rapped on the stairway wall. "Andy, come down here," he said, "There's a fella down here who wants to see you."

I thought it was one of the guys wanting to go play ball so I eased down the stairs and stepped out on the front porch.

There swaying back and forth in two rocking chairs, chewing tobacco, were Tom and Uncle Kirk.

"Somebody was in Uncle Kirk's corn last night and we want to know if you know anything about it," said Tom.

I looked out in the driveway and saw a corn shuck hanging out my front seat passenger window. We had shucked the corn on the way back to the campsite and thrown shucks out the window. It didn't take an Indian to follow the corn shuck trail and Uncle Kirk, about 85, with failing eyesight, easily followed the trail into our front yard.

I was caught red handed. There was no denying it when suddenly I had what I thought was a flash of brilliance.

"Well, I'll tell you one thing," I said, "I'll never loan my car to Bo again." Without another word I turned sharply and went back upstairs to bed. I didn't hear anything else about until about two weeks later when we were having dinner.

Tom looked over at my mom and said, "Hazel, I'd like to have some good fresh corn on the cob. Wonder where we could get some?"

"I hear Uncle Kirk Hatfield has some," she said.

Tom looked over at me and grinned and said, "Andy pass the corn, uh, bread please."

—◦◦◦◦◦◦◦—

The summer of '53 continued to be filled with unusual events.

During the summer I decided to become an entrepreneur. Bull Skeens who lived up at the head of Mate Creek had put in a television cable line. He charged each customer two dollars a month to be on the cable and each received three channels: ABC, NBC, and CBS.

Tom had run a line to the top of the mountain behind our house, but all we could get was NBC. Whenever we had a thunderstorm, tree limbs would fall on the line and the picture would go out. Usually Tom would send me and cousin Dan Kinder up the mountain to clear the line. I hated to do it because it seemed like a mile to the mountaintop. Dan and I would cuss all the way up.

Once when Dan and I climbed the mountain after a bad storm we passed an outcropping of rocks which reminded me of a story Tom had told me about the Devil's Backbone.

"Devil Anse joined the Confederate Army and became a First Lieutenant in Company A of the 45th Virginia Infantry.

"He was well known for his shootin' ability and could outshoot anybody. One day some Union soldiers trapped Devil on a high point in Logan County called the Devil's Backbone. The Union soldiers were firing at Devil from a ravine and were firing up toward a knob that towered over the mountain.

"Devil had them all pinned down with a single rifle and moved from one crevice to another picking off the Union soldiers one by one. The shootin' went on all day long.

"In the dark of night the Union soldiers picked up their dead and wounded and slipped away into the darkness."

"Is that the end?" I asked, wanting more.

"That's the end of the story," he said.

I believe he liked to tell them as much as I liked to hear them.

Now that Tom had signed on to the cable Dan and I wouldn't have to climb the mountain anymore. When the television went out it would be Bull's responsibility.

I'd heard that Bull wanted to sell the line. He had one hundred customers who paid two dollars a month so he was taking in two hundred dollars a month. I didn't see where he had any expenses once he got the line up.

With no money I decided I wanted to buy the line and go in the cable business. I found Bull in the back of his pickup rolling cable line. I'd heard Tom say that he was a real handyman and could fix anything.

"Hey Bull," I said, "I hear you might want to sell your cable line."

"Where did you hear that," he asked, without seeming to ask a question.

"Well, I just heard it somewhere. Do you want to sell it?" I asked.

"Yeah, I'll sell it."

"What do you want for it?"

"I'll take two thousand dollars for it."

"Two thousand dollars!" I exclaimed. "I thought you wanted to sell it."

"Two hundred dollars a month and in ten months you'll have your money back," he said.

"Yeah, if everybody pays."

"If they don't pay you just unhook 'em and they'll pay."

"I'll tell you what I'll do, Bull, I'll give you one thousand dollars next Friday and the other thousand at the end of five months."

He looked around toward his house as if his wife might not endorse the sale and then turned to me and said, "You have the thousand here by Friday and it's yours."

"I'll be here with the money."

That evening after supper I said, "Tom, what would it take for you to go my note at the Matewan Bank for two thousand dollars?"

After fully explaining the deal I told him I could pay off the loan at one-hundred fifty dollars a month and have it all paid back in thirteen months and then sit back and rake in two hundred a month.

He listened rather intently I thought and I felt like he might do it, but then he said, "Andy, you don't want to get involved in anything like that."

I knew there was no one else in the world I could get to help me raise the money so my plan to become a cable TV magnate never blossomed.

Five years later I was stationed at Fort Polk, Louisiana undergoing military police training, when I received a letter from Hazel. She noted that Tom had purchased a TV cable line from Bull Skeens for four thousand dollars.

Three years after that Tom sold the cable line to a man at Matewan for eighteen thousand dollars. I wrote him a note and told him that buying the cable line was my idea and I should share in the profits and he should send me seven thousand dollars which was fifty percent of the profit.

For the next forty years I reminded him from time to time that he owed me seven thousand dollars and asked when he was going to pay me.

"Well, now I would but I'm afraid Hazel would get mad. You know how she is."

—∿∿∿∿∿—

Most of the days in the summer of 1953 were boring, long and of little consequence. The sixteenth day of July was not one of those days.

The two tent meeting revivals were different and to some extent, memorable, but, no single day would be embellished upon my mind like Thursday, July the sixteenth.

The day started like any other day. I woke up about eight o'clock and lay in bed until about nine-thirty. I went downstairs and put two pieces of Sunbeam light bread in the toaster and when they popped up I covered them lavishly with homemade apple butter Aunt Nannie had made and devoured them with a glass of milk.

I was ready for the day but nothing was going to happen. There was little chance of any kind of romance. I had no money to play poker. I'd searched through Hazel's purse the night before and the pocket where she kept her change was empty except for three pennies. I didn't take 'em because if I got in a game and lost the first game I would be busted. I didn't dare take a bill.

After the toast and apple butter I went out and sat down on the front porch steps. It was a hazy morning but you could tell it was going to be clear later in the day. No one was in sight except Tater Bug who was sitting in the front yard with Little Beaver. They couldn't be discussing anything of consequence because they didn't know anything of consequence. I wondered what they could be talking about but decided I didn't care. Whatever it was they were discussing would be so childish and unimportant it wouldn't matter. They were probably talking about bugs or dogs or something.

It was time to go to the store. Aunt Ella, Tom's youngest sister, worked at the store but had to go to the doctor at ten-thirty and Tom had asked me to mind the store until she returned.

By noon I'd only had two or three customers and hadn't sold five dollars worth of groceries. I wished Ella would hurry and get back. Anything I could do would be better than minding the store.

Just after noon two girls came in. I'd never seen them before. They looked to be about eighteen and weren't very pretty. At least not pretty enough to flirt with.

They'd pulled up in a 1947 Plymouth with Kentucky tags. The Plymouth had seen its better days. The right back fender was missing, exposing a bald, half-inflated tire.

The black-haired one had a pair of khaki shorts and a red halter-top. She was less ugly than the other one who wore a pair of blue jeans and a tee shirt. The tee shirt was mostly flat with only a slight protrusion. She had a harsher look than the younger one. Perhaps she was mad because her breasts hadn't grown with the rest of her body. I assumed she was the leader.

"Gimme two cokes," she said, and reached for her purse. It was then I realized it wasn't a purse but a brown paper bag.

My first thought was that the bag contained sandwiches or something for lunch. Her hand came out of the bag with a pistol in it and she pointed it straight at my head. It appeared to be a snub-nose, thirty-eight special just like the one Tom had.

"Give me your damn money you son-of-a-bitch," she said.

I knew from the tone of her voice she meant business. I didn't want to give her the money but I didn't want to get shot and maybe killed for one hundred thirty-five dollars. I had counted it when Ella left so I'd know how much I started with so I could tell Tom how much I had taken in.

Several thoughts raced through my mind simultaneously but the overwhelming one was how I was going to tell Tom that I had let two girls rob me and take all the store's money. That thought scared me more than getting shot.

I walked behind the counter and opened the cash register and removed the bills not bothering with the change which probably was another twenty dollars. I laid the bills on the counter top and stepped back. The gun was still pointing directly at my head.

If I had been more than sixteen and if I had had any sense at all, I would have given her the money and done nothing. There was no way they could escape out of the hollow.

But, at sixteen the most important thing in the world to a boy is his pride. If they got away with the money my cousins would torment me forever.

They would sing, "two little girls took Andy Dock's money," and laugh and laugh. I would never be able to live it down. They would sing, "Andy Dock is a scaredy cat, Andy Dock's a scaredy cat."

The older one picked up the money and stuffed it into her blue jeans.

"Let's go, Millie," she said, and they moved to the door.

Why did she say her name, I wondered. Is she that dumb or was it a trick to throw me off?

The younger one went out and just as the older one stepped through the door I jumped over the counter and in two steps crashed through the screen door knocking her to the ground. I was on top of her in a flash and hit her as hard as I could square in the face.

The pistol had jarred loose and was just under the storefront. I grabbed it and threw it as far back under the store as I could.

The younger one started crying and knelt over her friend.

"You killed her!" she cried.

"She's not dead. That blood's just coming from a busted nose," I said, hoping she wasn't really dead.

Within a few seconds the older one was on her feet holding her bloody nose. The blood was running through her fingers and down her flat tee shirt.

"Gimme that money," I said as if I were going to hit her again.

She took it from her blue jeans and threw it on the ground. Part of it was covered with blood but it would still spend.

"I guess you all know your ass is going to jail for robbery and attempted murder," I said.

"We didn't 'tempt to kill nobody," said the younger one. "There weren't no bullets in that gun."

The gun was under the store and I wasn't going to crawl under there and get it and I couldn't send the younger one after it because if it had bullets she would shoot me for sure.

The store sat on two cinder blocks and crawling under it was a tight squeeze. I'd have to wait until Ella got back.

I didn't know what to do next. They were both crying. I felt a little sorry for them. I wasn't afraid of them anymore and for whatever reason I'll never know I told them to come back in the store.

I gave the younger one a rag we used to wipe the counter top and told her to clean her buddy's face. I gave them the cokes they had ordered earlier.

I stood there looking at them for a few minutes and they looked awful pitiful. Every now and then they took a sip of coke and looked at me. I hated to see them go to jail.

"What if I let you all go?" I asked. Would you ever do something like this again?"

Their eyes lit up and the younger one stood up and said, "Praise Jesus, I'll never do nothin' like this again in my life if you'll let us go."

"I'll tell you what I'm going to do," I said. "You all get in your car and go back where you come from and let this be a lesson to you the next time you want to rob somebody."

As they walked out the door the younger one turned and asked, "Do you want us to pay for the cokes?"

"Get the hell out of here," I said. "The cokes are on me."

A few minutes after they were gone Aunt Ella got back.

"Anything happen?" she asked.

No, just another boring, long, hot summer day in July, I said, but I knew I would have to explain why the green in the cash register had turned red. But I wanted to wait and tell Tom about it first. He would tell me if I had made the right decisions.

And, if I hadn't, I had their license plate number and the gun was under the store.

As it turned out the license plates had been stolen from a car in Delbarton. The two girls apparently disappeared from the face of the earth. The Plymouth was never seen again and there was really nothing to collaborate my story.

Maybe God had sent two angels or devils to test my courage. But, that night when Tom counted the blood-stained money and I crawled out from under the store with an unloaded thirty-eight special, I knew it had really happened.

After I told Tom the story he never did really tell me if I had made the right decisions. I know he believed me and he was probably just glad I hadn't been shot.

Whether he believed me or not, he cleaned that thirty-eight and two months later sold it to a man over on Beech Creek for a hundred-fifty dollars. At least that more than paid for the two cokes I had given those bitches. I wanted to tell him half of it should be mine because I was the one who captured the gun, but I didn't.

The sixteenth day of July, 1953, made me realize that long, hot, boring summer days weren't all that bad. I didn't get bored again for two weeks.

—᷉᷉᷉᷉᷉᷉—

Three days before my senior year began, Evangeline McCoy came in the store. I was engaged in a Captain Marvel comic book, which immediately seemed childish. I quickly dropped it under the counter top, hoping she hadn't seen it.

Vangie had been Homecoming Queen at Matewan High when I was in junior high school at Red Jacket. She rode Tom's school bus during my seventh and eighth grade years. When I boarded the bus at Tom's store Vangie was already on the bus and someone was always in the seat beside her. Only once in two years did I get to sit beside her on the way to Red Jacket.

There was always one seat available beside Ellie Marcum and I usually took it. Ellie weighed at least 220 pounds and took up most of two seats. I only weighed about 125 pounds so I fit easily on the half seat not inhabited by Ellie's thighs.

If there was an empty seat before Ellie's aisle I would take it, but I never passed her because I didn't want to hurt her feelings. All my friends teased me about Ellie being my sweetheart. I think she had a crush on me but I understood because I had one on Evangeline.

Vangie was absolutely beautiful. She had long, black hair which always seemed to shine as if she had just washed it. Her dark eyebrows arched in the center making a striking frame for two sparkling green eyes. Her nose was just one of those perfect noses and fit perfectly above two luscious, red full lips.

She may have been a McCoy but I would have eagerly betrayed Great Grandfather Ellison, Uncle Devil Anse, Father Tom C. and all the Hatfields and Chafins in my family tree to have her. But I was sure she regarded me as just a young school kid, if at all. If Roseanna McCoy had been half as pretty as Vangie I could well understand why Johnse had swum Tug River to hold her.

She was nineteen and I was sixteen, and she seemed so mature and sure of herself. She would graduate from college when I graduated from high school. She made me feel like I was in the second grade.

"Hi Andy, I really like your car," she said.

I summoned all the courage I had and said, "Let me take you for a ride in it."

Tom had bought me a black 1932 model T Ford convertible with a wheel on the back, and a rumble seat and it was a real beauty. He paid $300 for it.

"Okay," she said.

I was suddenly scared. What if she had somehow heard the story about the cornfield. Surely Hammer hadn't told anyone. What would she say if she knew I had briefly seen her bare backside?

Suddenly it occurred to me that she had always been nice to me. She always said hello or smiled whenever we saw each other. Maybe, I thought, she doesn't think I'm too young for her.

My voice cracked when I asked, "When would you like to do it?"

"Anytime," she said. "What about this evening?"

It was a balmy August evening. I washed the Model T until it sparkled. It was a perfect evening for a ride. I was nervous. What had I gotten myself into? Was she just playing with me? What would I say?

Well, it wasn't a date, I thought, she was just being friendly with me. Then why am I so nervous? I'm not nervous, I thought, I'm down right scared to death.

At seven o'clock I pulled the shiny Model T in front of her house. I was worried I had put too much of Tom's aftershave on. I wasn't old enough to shave but I raked Tom's razor across my face just to be sure.

Old Man McCoy and Mrs. McCoy were sitting on the front porch. I had the strongest urge to drive away but I'd come too far.

I made myself get out of the car and walked toward the porch. "Where's Vangie?" I asked, as if it were the most normal thing in the world.

"How are you, Andy?" asked Mrs. McCoy, and before I could answer she said, "Vangie's gone to Matewan on a date."

"Oh well, she said she liked my car and I told her I'd take her for ride in it sometime," I said, trying to sound as if it were a spur-of-the-moment idea and not really very important.

We talked for a few minutes but I don't remember what was said. All I could think of was her telling me to be there at seven o'clock. That bitch, I thought. She was playing with me. I felt sick to my stomach. I'll never speak to that bitch again.

Trying my best to be nonchalant I said goodbye to the McCoys and walked to the car.

The damn thing wouldn't start. I cranked it until the battery was almost gone. What if Vangie had been there, I thought. What if she had gotten in this car and the damn thing wouldn't start. That would have been more embarrassing than her not being there.

I had to leave the car in front of the McCoy's house. I told them I would come and get it in the morning. They were very nice about it.

As I walked out of their front yard toward the highway I noticed their corn was withering. It hadn't withered as much as my pride. I hadn't felt so embarrassed since I had that little innocuous expiration of gas in first grade writing class.

Nine

FROM THE TIME THE FIRST WAVE OF PIONEERS challenged the mountains in the early seventeenth century until the Industrial Revolution hit America, the region remained largely unchanged.

Neither the Revolutionary War nor the Civil War had managed to change the lives of Appalachians significantly.

With the onset of the Civil War, Appalachians were divided in their allegiance. My great-great uncle, Devil Anse, had led a troop of Confederates, but slavery was not the primary cause of the division, nor the reason for West Virginia breaking away from Virginia to form a separate state.

The concept of slavery was alien to the nature of the mountaineer. The underlying cause of the division was socio-economic and political.

It seemed that before I could turn around, the summer had vanished. Although each day seemed to move slowly, the summer had slipped away.

During August, I decided to go out for the football team. At five feet eleven, I weighed one hundred fifty pounds, but was fairly compact and had good leg strength. I secretly believed, of course, that I would make the team easily. For once I wasn't relegated to the second team. I made the third team.

The first few days of practice were brutal. The coaches put me in at fullback in their single-wing offense where I was to serve as "practice meat" for the first and second team defenses.

I made the team mostly because I was another body needed for practice and, of course, quickly found a home on the third team. Not having played my sophomore and junior years, I knew I would only see action when the Tigers had a commanding lead.

In the sixth game of the year I got my chance against an out-manned Chapmansville team. I ran the ball well and had one or two tackles and felt good about getting into the action.

Cousin Jack had responsibility for calling the *Williamson Daily News* with game details and after the game at the sock hop, he told me I had played well. "I gave you a good write-up," he said.

"Yeah, good," I said, without too much thought.

When the newspaper came out the next day I was mortified. According to Jack's report I had played a super game on defense, made touchdown-saving tackles and been a key to the Tigers' forty-point victory.

Without doubt, I would be recruited by Alabama, Notre Dame and Michigan. I was totally humiliated.

How could I face the team on Monday and what could I say?

I hid out for the entire weekend and on Monday morning stayed in bed.

Hazel kept calling upstairs, "Andy, get up. You're going to be late for school."

I didn't move.

"Andy, what's wrong with you?" she yelled. "Get up!"

Finally up the stairs she came demanding to know why I hadn't got out of bed.

"I'm sick as a dog," I lied.

"What's wrong with you?"

"I feel like I'm going to throw up," I said, as pitiful as I could.

"Do you want to go to the doctor?"

"No, I'll be all right if I can lay here awhile."

I hadn't lied about being sick to miss school since the fifth grade when I was afraid I was going to fail a math test, but I just couldn't face the team.

As soon as the school bus had gone I got up and drooped around the house and recovered from my illness about ten o'clock. If I stayed sick too long she might try to stop me from playing ball when everyone got in from school.

Tuesday morning came early and I knew I couldn't play sick again. I had to face the music.

At school, much to my relief, nobody mentioned the game write-up all day. I was extremely thankful. If I could get through football practice without anybody saying anything it might be all right. Maybe nobody had paid any attention to the article, or, maybe and even better, perhaps I had really played good.

At practice, the third team ran offensive plays against the first team and I was taking a beating. As I tried to dash through the line I was smothered and my head was driven into the ground by two large defensive tackles.

I was slow to get up and Coach Miller in a sarcastic tone said, "get up, hero." To make it worse he looked over at Coach Wetzel and asked, "Did you see that?" referring to the game write-up.

Coach Wetzel nodded his head, but thankfully didn't say anything.

I got up and went back to the huddle and asked if I could run the ball again. My nose had started to bleed and I was exhausted, but I kept driving into the line and kept getting killed.

Each time I was driven into the ground, I kept hoping the punishment I was taking would somehow make up for the undeserving praise of the newspaper article.

The coaches, who weren't exactly all-star practitioners of child psychology, hardly spoke to me the rest of the season and never let me run another single down. But, I continued to attend practice and by the final game had found a permanent home on the third team because we didn't have enough players for a fourth team.

Cousin Jack continued to phone in game details but with an added emphasis on fact. He never mentioned the article to me, and I wondered if the coaches had chewed him out. Perhaps he understood the agony I felt or perhaps he never thought about it. I never knew and never mentioned the game again.

Throughout my senior year, I persistently resisted Tom's pleadings to study. It seemed my generation paid little attention and like many of my friends and cousins, I would have dropped out of school had it not been for his insistence.

Years later, I could still remember his words, "Andy, you can be somebody if you'll listen to me."

I agreed but continued to avoid any pursuit of educational excellence or to establish any lifelong goals. Perhaps the economy and environment of the coalfields left us with little ambition or hope that we could ever be successful in anything.

But I knew Tom's goal very well. It was to some day be high sheriff of Mingo County, and in 1972 he would embark upon a rather circuitous route to that goal.

—————

At ten o'clock the morning after Vangie stood me up I walked through her yard toward my car. As I neared the car she came out on the porch wearing a sleeveless red shirt and a pair of short shorts. As I had expected she had legs all the way up to her tail and they were extremely well proportioned.

I stopped and looked at her and she looked at me. After a few seconds I wondered which one of us would look away first. It wasn't going to be me. It seemed like we were flirting, but surely she wouldn't flirt with me.

Without looking away she said, "I really didn't think you would come by. I'm sorry I wasn't here."

"Oh, that's all right, the car wouldn't start anyway," I said, overjoyed that she seemed repentant.

"Are you mad at me?" she asked.

"I don't know," I replied.

"When will you know?"

I felt like she was getting the upper hand but for some reason I didn't mind.

"What can I do to make it up to you?" she asked

"Who did you have a date with?"

"Just a friend I go to school with."

"Is he your boyfriend?"

"No, he's just a friend."

"Do you have a boyfriend?"

"I date a boy at school but we're mostly friends."

"Is he in love with you?"

"Probably."

"Are you in love with him?"

"No. What can I do to make it up to you?"

I stared at her for just a few seconds and blurted, "What about a kiss?" and was immediately embarrassed at how silly it sounded.

"Okay," she replied. "Do you want to come in?"

Where was her mom, I thought? I knew Mr. McCoy was at work. He worked at Number Seventeen Mine and Tom said he hadn't missed a shift in eight years. But, where was Mrs. McCoy?

As if reading my mind she said, "Mom has gone to Matewan."

I walked toward the porch. My heart was pounding. I was scared but not scared enough not to go in. My knees were so weak I barely made it up the porch steps.

She opened the door and I walked in. Three steps inside I stopped and turned toward her. She stopped and we stood there looking at each other.

"Do you want it now?" she asked.

I wondered if she was talking about the kiss or had something more in mind.

"Yes," I stammered.

She opened her arms as if I were supposed to walk into them. I did.

The Model T started on the first turn of the key.

The political "machine" was headed by the county Democratic chairman and included all courthouse employees, liquor store workers, highway department personnel and everyone employed under the political patronage system and all their relatives. To oppose the machine-backed slate of candidates in Mingo meant immediate and certain loss of a job for the dissenter and his relatives.

No one had ever beaten the machine, but Tom, after more than twenty years as constable, justice of the peace and county court clerk, had made a host of friends throughout the county and decided to battle the machine.

He filed his candidacy for the office of sheriff in January 1972 and proceeded to round up and head a full slate of candidates picked to oppose the machine-backed incumbents.

The campaigning began in January and grew into a fever pitch by the May ninth election date. Charges, counter charges, threats, lies and promises filled the air. Initially the race had been taken rather lightly by the machine, but by mid-March had blossomed into a real dogfight.

I was convinced that if anyone could beat the machine, Tom could do it. His natural instinct for politics and campaigning and his ability to establish kinship with any voter in Mingo County via his double cousin status with the Hatfields had the machine worried, but they remained confident. After all, no one had ever beaten the machine.

Original campaign poster from author's collection.

From time to time during the campaign, I would ask him if he was going to win.

"Well, I don't know," he would say. "It don't look too good. They've got all their people in the election houses and they can steal two thousand votes."

He was regarded by political leaders as a tough cam-
paigner and each of his 160 pounds would work until the last
vote was cast. His philosophy was to work until the polls
closed as if one more vote would decide the election.

Even when he was on the losing side, he never became
angry at his opponents. "Your worst enemy this election may
be your strongest ally the next time," he would say. And in
Mingo County, it often happened exactly that way.

"It don't look too good," he would repeat. "But don't
worry about it, it's only an election."

I wondered how he could take it so lightly. I was torn all
to pieces. I knew his lifelong goal was to be high sheriff but he
was acting like it wasn't that important. Perhaps, I thought, he
knew he was going to lose and was trying to spare me from
being too disappointed. The thought crushed me.

I thought about the time when I had gone to the movie
next door at my neighbor's theatre. I was twelve and had sat
beside a girl from Straight Fork, a small community about
three miles up the hollow from our house.

Our sitting next together was quite benign but when I
went to the lobby for popcorn I was accosted by an older man
in his late thirties. It seemed he had a crush on the girl I was
sitting with and without any warning he hit me in the face with
his fist.

I fell to the floor but quickly jumped up and ran home.
Tom was sitting on the front porch and saw me hobble in crying.

"What happened?" he asked.

"Some old man hit me and knocked me down," I said.

He shot up out of his rocking chair and headed for the
theatre with me right on his heels.

The man was still there.

"Did you hit him?" he asked.

Before he could answer Tom hit him smack-dab in the
jaw and down he went.

He got up and Tom greeted him with another shot to the chin and down he went again. He got up two or three times and Tom knocked him down each time.

And then we went back to our front porch. That would teach that sucker to be careful who he hit the next time, I thought.

On May 9, 1972, the polls closed at seven-thirty. I had waited anxiously all day, alternately convincing myself that Tom couldn't possibly win, and then that he might pull off the upset.

At eight-thirty, the Williamson radio station began broadcasting the returns. Precincts in Williamson would report first and would give an indication of how the vote would go countywide. If the Williamson precincts came in heavily against us, we could assume the election was lost.

I was greatly encouraged when the Courthouse, the first Williamson precinct, reported. For sheriff of Mingo County, Chafin 113, Wellman 114. My encouragement was short lived when the second precinct, Williamson Hollow, reported Chafin 36, Wellman 200. The Williamson Hollow Precinct was where the black voters lived and could be expected to vote the machine slate. Perhaps he could make it up in other places.

After all seven Williamson precincts were in, the vote was Chafin 847, Wellman 694. The machine had lost the big Williamson District, but their strength was out in the hollows and up the creeks. But, still I was heartened and knew that Tom had a chance.

As the vote came in from precincts around the county, the lead changed hands several times. It was apparent that the race was going down to the wire, perhaps down to the last precinct reporting.

With the vote at 4,204 for Chafin and 3,867 for Wellman, two precincts remained to be reported. Unfortunately, they were the two precincts in the opponent's home district and would surely wipe out the 337 vote lead and cost Black Tom the election.

I was sure the Dingess Precinct would delay reporting their vote until they knew how many votes were needed to win. The two precincts usually reported about 400 votes for the machine and about 20 for the opposition. I had very little hope that the 337 lead would hold out.

The next to last precinct finally reported. The announcer said, "The Breeden Precinct Chafin 33, Wellman 80." The lead was down to 290 with the big Dingess precinct still to be reported.

Finally, the Dingess Precinct reported Chafin 19, Wellman 320. The race was lost by eleven votes. The machine had again proven its invincibility. I was sick at my stomach. Tom had worked so hard and had had the election stolen. There was no justice in Mingo County, I thought.

As in every election in Mingo County, widespread charges of irregularities and vote fraud were rampant. I heard someone say the Dingess precinct had two voting machines but used only one, and that it was physically impossible to cast on one machine the number of votes reported.

Unbelievably, two precincts in the Gilbert District had allowed voters to vote until ten-thirty p.m., three hours after the official closing time. Tom, having lost the two precincts by a total of 68 votes, pursued the matter in circuit court.

To my great surprise, to the great surprise of my family, to the great surprise, I'm sure, of my dead ancestors who obviously were forced to vote the machine slate, and to the surprise of every person in Mingo County who had voted for Chafin for sheriff, the circuit judge threw out two Gilbert precincts and awarded the sheriff's office to Black Tom.

The machine had been beaten by their own unbelief that any judge would challenge their wrongdoing. The final vote, Chafin 4,076, Wellman 4,016.

I was ecstatic. The old machine had been beaten and a new machine was about to be born which four years later would carry Black Tom to a commanding 2,500-vote margin in his re-election to the office of sheriff.

Three minutes after Tom took the oath of office for sheriff, his opponent was sworn in as County Clerk, the office Tom had vacated to become sheriff. It could only happen in wild, wonderful Mingo County, West Virginia.

—✍✍✍✍—

A few years after Tom's passing I found the following letter in some of his old photos. I thought it was fairly well accurate.

I've also got a leftover election story for you. I was given to understand that it's absolutely true.

Some years ago, I'm reliably informed, not long after a hotly fought, closely contested election, a newly elected sheriff in Mingo County got a telephone call at this home late on Saturday night.

"Sheriff," said the caller, "this here is Chief Deputy Wallace Baisden down at the jail. Sheriff, I hate to bother you when you're at home and all but we've got a fellow down here we picked up just a while ago for drunk and disorderly, resisting arrest, causing a public disturbance and a few other odds and ends. Sheriff, he's claiming he's some kind of relative of yours and I thought well, maybe we better let you know."

"Who is he?" the sheriff asked.

The deputy supplied a name.

"I can't place him," said the sheriff.

"Well," said the deputy, "he's pretty dern insistent, Sheriff, that he's some of your kin and he keeps hollering that we can't do this to him."

"All right," said the sheriff. "I'll come down."

When he arrived at the jail a little later, the deputy led him back to the cell where the prisoner was slumped on a cot. The sheriff examined the man closely. He did look vaguely familiar.

"Now listen here, young fellow," the sheriff said, "I hear you've been telling these deputies that you and I are some-ways related. Suppose you tell me–just how is it we're supposed to be kin to each other?"

"Sheriff," replied the prisoner, "I don't rightly recollect exactly myself. But when you and me met up while you was out lookin' for votes right before the election, you explained it to me just absolutely perfect."

You gotta vote for kinfolks, right?

Ten

IN JANUARY OF MY SENIOR YEAR IN HIGH SCHOOL, the Rose Bowl was broadcast in color for the first time. In February in Pittsburgh, Pennsylvania, Salk's vaccine was given to children for the first time and in March CBS introduced "The Morning Show" to compete with NBC's "Today" show."

April saw the National Basketball Association adopt the 24-second shot clock rule and in May Stan Musial hit five homeruns in a doubleheader.

Such trifles of history could hardly compare and certainly not compete with the enrollment of Julie Smith at Magnolia High School.

I saw her the first day of school during my senior year and was in love the moment I saw her. She was the most beautiful girl I had ever seen. Peach-blonde hair, cascading over her shoulders, struggled toward perfectly proportioned thighs.

Creamy-white skin, enhanced by a natural blush in her cheeks, surrounded lips, which looked as if they might taste like ripe, red August raspberries. An ever-so-slight space between her two front teeth hinted not at imperfection, but distinction.

Her name was Julie. Julie Smith. She was all I imagined a girl could be. I was captivated, filled with an urgency to be where I thought she might appear. I couldn't get her out of my mind.

I waited for three days before an opportunity to meet her occurred. I wasn't going to wait any longer. As we passed in the auditorium between classes, I reached out my hand, and said "Hello," and told her my name. "Hello," she said, "I'm

Julie Smith," as if a little embarrassed at my unexpected introduction.

"Where did you go to school last year?" I asked.

"We moved here in July from Charlotte, North Carolina," she said.

"You're very beautiful," I blurted. "Would you like to go to the dance with me after the game Friday?"

"Thank you, but I don't think I can," she said.

"Are you going to the game?" I asked.

"Yes, I think so."

"Are you going to the dance?"

"I don't know if I can," she replied.

"Well, if you do, would you save me a dance?"

"Okay," she said.

"Nice to meet you," I said. "See you later."

"It was nice to meet you," she said and smiled.

I wasn't sure, but I thought she was pleased at my invitation. At least she would be thinking about it and probably would tell all her sophomore friends that a senior had asked her to the dance. It would be tough waiting for Friday. I should have said more, I thought.

After the game, I waited a little while before going to the dance. I saw her as soon as I walked in, but acted as if I didn't. I danced with two or three girls and tried to act as if I didn't know she was there. I knew exactly where she was, but never let her see my frequent glances.

When the right slow music started I quickly walked toward her. "Is this my dance?" I asked.

She smiled and reached for my hand.

She felt good. She smelled good. She looked good. I was enthralled with her, but tried to appear to be the cool upperclassman.

Midway through the song I pulled back and looked at her and asked, "May I have all your dances for the rest of your life?" I thought the shock treatment would be just the thing for the beautiful, young sophomore.

She leaned forward, hiding her eyes from me and whispered, " Why?"

"Because you're beautiful and you fill my heart with spring," I said.

She smiled and leaned her head back on my shoulder, but said nothing.

When the music stopped she pulled away and said, "Thank you."

"Thank you," I replied. "The pleasure was entirely mine."

As I walked back to the other side of the room, I felt a little silly. It hadn't gone too well, I thought. She probably thought I was nuts.

I didn't dance with her again and didn't see her until Monday. She needed time to think about what I had said, I reasoned.

Between classes on Monday the hallway was very crowded, but I waited until I saw her. I reached for her arm and gently pulled her to the wall. She was willing. "What about all those dances for rest of your life?" I asked.

To my surprise, she said. "They're all yours."

"Why?" I asked.

"Because I put spring in your heart," she smiled.

I continued down the hallway with a spring in my step, sure that I was truly in love. But it didn't last. It never did at sixteen. But it would be my most memorable childhood romance.

—◦◦◦◦◦◦—

Except, of course, for Evangeline. Vangie was the epitome of womanhood. I often thought about that day in August when she opened her arms and invited me in. Her red shirt seemed to dissolve as it dropped to the floor. Her nipples pointed sharply forward as if seeking immediate attention.

As her arms spread and invited me in, her hands dropped and deftly moved her shorts down her thighs exposing an array of black silky, curly hair meant to be seen only by the gods.

It was the feeling you get after the sun bursts out from the clouds. The thrill you might feel when you hear "bombs away," "Gentlemen, start your engines," "They're off," or circle the bases after hitting a grand slam in the bottom of the ninth with your team down three runs.

That day I believed she felt something strong for me, but as the years went by my illusion evaporated. I wanted to be her knight in shining armor but I was too young to be a knight and if I'd had shining armor I wouldn't have known how to put it on. Perhaps I was only a teenage diversion. By my third year in college she had two daughters and a coalminer husband who had deserted her for a sixteen-year-old girl from Hazard, Kentucky. She never finished her last year of college. Soon after her husband left she joined hundreds of others on the Mingo County welfare rolls. She just seemed to give up. Perhaps it was our culture. But, I never forgot her and the warm August day when she let me for the first time experience the marvelous joys of the flesh.

It became one of my most joyful teenage memories and remained with me, as a youthful, all-American, wholesome experience untainted by guilt, sorrow or regret.

In early June of 1954, Cousin Jack and I departed for Concord College in Athens, West Virginia. As we waited in the back seat of Tom's 1953 Chevrolet for the three-hour trip, I had an uneasy feeling. I sensed a shadow was beginning to blot out an important part of my life.

The stories about Devil Anse and my great-grandfather Ellison and how their lives had become a part of American history flashed before me.

I remembered how hard I had laughed on the hot summer afternoon when Bo and Bennie dashed naked around the schoolhouse. I could still almost smell the terrible odor of John and Junebug's gas war. And, I could hear the cornstalks being crunched behind me in Vangie's cornfield as I fled for safety.

But, those days were gone forever now and it saddened me. Although I was only seventeen, the thoughts of Devil Anse and my ancestors kept coming back to me.

I was becoming aware of my mortality and, for the first time I could ever remember, I realized that one's life was only a small tick in the endless clock of time and that it would soon be time to die, even if I lived another hundred years.

I wanted to feel the quiet in Matewan just five minutes before Smilin' Sid shot Albert Felts in the back of the head and then smell the smoke of the gunfire as it enveloped the town.

I wanted to see Johnse Hatfield wading out of Tug River at Steptown to embrace Roseanna and see the look on his face when the McCoys surrounded him.

I wanted to see Devil Anse riding his horse Fred at the head of the posse as they raced to rescue Johnse.

I wanted to see Smilin' Sid as he walked up the McDowell County courthouse steps moments before the Baldwin-Felts people gunned him down.

I wanted to see the faces of the townspeople as they watched Bo and Hornie dash naked around the school.

I wanted to see Julie Smith's face when she said I could have all the dances in her future.

I wanted to see Great Grandfather Ellison as he sauntered up to the polling place with his wide-brim hat and see the knife wounds inflicted by the McCoy brothers.

I wanted to see Evangeline come out on her front porch and hear her say she was sorry for standing me up.

I was glad I would always have these things with me. I could pull them up in my mind in black and white or living Technicolor any time I wished.

The Matewan High School class of 1954 was now history but the year would be memorable in American history. Joe DiMaggio would marry Marilyn Monroe, Harvard doctors would perform the first kidney transplant operation, Roger Bannister would become the first person to break the four-minute mile and Willie Mays would lead the New York Giants to a World Series victory. Two of our classmates would go on to play major league baseball. Jack Hatfield would pitch for the Atlanta Braves and Rodney "Doc" Edwards would catch for and manage the Cleveland Indians. For two kids in such a small school in such a small town in such a small county to make major league baseball teams was just awesome. As far as I know, none of the rest of us would achieve anything as noteworthy.

As Tom finally came out the walkway, Mrs. Montgomery and her husband Carl pulled in beside us in their 1953 Buick. Mr. Montgomery eased from his car and began talking with Tom. He was likely trying to get Tom's support for two members of the Mingo County School Board who were up for re-election. In a little while we heard Tom say, "Well, I've got to take these boys to Concord College."

Mrs. Montgomery leaned her familiar gray head out the window and in the most serious manner remarked, "They ought to do good. They've just had three years of rest at Matewan High School."

I wondered if she was still mad at me over the anecdote caper.

Jack and I looked at each other and grinned. No reply would be worthy of such a classic statement.

As Tom pulled away, I knew a chapter in my life had ended. Perhaps, I thought, it might be the best chapter of all.

As we pulled out of New Town toward Red Jacket, my thoughts suddenly focused on Hugh O'Keefe. I felt ashamed that I had thought his life was unimportant. He might have been the most successful man I would ever know.

In God's eyes he might have been an Angel. The fact that nobody in London or New York knew that he had ever existed was not necessarily a true measurement of his worth. The value of his life could only be measured by God.

I felt sorry about my assessment of Hugh's life and ashamed of my audacity in considering his life meaningless.

If Hugh was a failure then everyone I knew in New Town was a failure as well. They worked in the mines and took care of their families as best they could. That was honorable and good. They were not failures.

Who am I, I thought, to judge any man's worth?

And, who was I to insult Melody about her clothes that day in the seventh grade? If I had been in her circumstances how would I have felt if someone had commented on my clothes?

I felt sorry about all the bad things I had done in my first sixteen years of life.

I felt a strong desire to ask everyone I had offended to forgive me. We all lived in dire circumstances. How ridiculous of us to feel that those who lived at the mouth of the creek were more socially prominent than those who lived at the head of the creek.

As the miles ticked away my sorrow quickly faded and the cockiness of youth slowly returned. We were seventeen and invincible and although we were sure we already knew practically everything that was worth knowing, everyone was saying a college degree had become essential if you were going to find a good job and stay out of the coal mines.

During my first two weeks at Concord College I realized that the world didn't begin at New Town and only reach to Matewan, West Virginia.

After four weeks I realized that a whole new world existed beyond Mingo County. I knew my childhood had ended and I had stepped into a future full of endless potential and possibility.

THE END

The Characters

TOM PASSED AWAY IN APRIL, 1997, just a few days short of his eighty-sixth birthday. Governor Cecil Underwood, Senate President Earl Tomblin, and several state legislators and officials attended his funeral. I think about him a lot and hope to hear the "cow story" one more time in Heaven.

Hazel still lives in Williamson and up until a few years ago continued painting beautiful acrylic paintings. She submitted two paintings to the Huntington, West Virginia Art Gallery but when a Huntington doctor bought one for eight hundred dollars she was devastated. She vowed never to sell another painting and ten of her best now adorn the walls of my Lebanon, Virginia home.

Ms. Bea who gave us those beautiful Bible stories each week, now sleeps with the angels and must be quite beautiful in the sight of God.

Julie Smith moved back to North Carolina after graduating from high school and was never heard from again.

Bennie Horn got his vocabulary right, graduated from Marshall University with honors and became a high school English teacher.

Jack settled in Cleveland, Ohio where he is a manufacturer's representative and owns his own successful company. He winters in Fort Pierce, Florida in one of his various condos.

Labella Testerman Hatfield left Matewan after Smilin' Sid was gunned down by the Baldwin-Felts people on the steps of the McDowell County courthouse in Welch, West Virginia and the last time Arbutus heard from her she was dancing on Bourbon Street in New Orleans.

Junebug Simpkins married a McCoy girl from Pikeville and would have lived happily ever after had she not run off with a Bible salesman from Louisville.

Old Man Beecher Mounts lived fifteen years after his outhouse was tumbled into Mate Creek. He never found out who did it.

Bo settled in the family's old homeplace and still enjoys needling his friends and cousins. Between needling sessions he visits his 400-acre farm in Lexington, Kentucky.

Josh was killed in an auto accident at the age of 26. His search for a girlfriend never bore fruit. I have serious doubts he's in Heaven.

Hammer worked in the coal mines and retired with two black lungs in 1987.

Melody married right out of high school and raised four fine boys and somehow got better looking as she aged and is now out of the beyond ugly group. God is merciful.

Johnny Varney married an older woman with two children and they moved into his Mom's house. After his bride had three more children his Mom gave him the house and moved into the public housing project on Vangie's cornfield.

Little Beaver went to Venezuela and became a leading jockey. He never weighed more that 112 pounds and was down to 98 when his horse threw him and broke his neck.

Beulah Jane Mitchell – her leg never healed properly and she had to walk with a cane the rest of her life. She told everyone she met that God had cured her arthritis and she didn't care about her crippled leg.

Scotty still lives at Low Gap. I see him at our high school reunions every three years. He's still the jolly, nice fellow he was in high school.

Biff Johnson briefly pursued a boxing career but after losing his first five fights by knockouts, went to work in the coalmines. He didn't seem to have a glass jaw in the ninth grade. Perhaps I had a weak punch.

Vangie married four times and is reportedly searching for lucky number five. She still looks good for a girl of 68. Her dad's cornfield is now home to a low-income public housing project. Hugh O'Keefe's children all live in the project. I saw Vangie at the Matewan Bank during our 1997 high school reunion. She invited me to come up and see her. I thanked her but didn't go. At our ages another visit couldn't possibly live up to the one we had in the fifties. And, I certainly had no desire to be lucky number five although I had to admit she was the best looking woman of 68 I'd ever seen.

Adele enjoyed a successful political career in Ohio but while being groomed by the Democratic hierarchy for a high political office contracted some type of new social disease and met an untimely death at the age of forty-five. I assume her liberal outlook regarding lovemaking led to her early demise.

I went back to school after a stint in the Army and graduated from Morris Harvey College in Charleston, thirteen years after Jack and I left for Concord. I've spent the past thirty-four years in a job which gives me the opportunity to help improve the quality of life for the Appalachian people whom I dearly love.

The author, Andrew Chafin

A Final Word

No greater conflict occurs than when a man, in order to survive economically, must uproot his family from their comfortable ancestral home to a strange, new insensitive urban environment

As I became a teenager in the 1950's all of Appalachia, especially central Appalachia, was showing signs of economic and social distress. As the problems deepened my people in Mingo County joined two million others in a massive outward migration to urban centers.

They left in the 1950's but came back in the 1980's and 1990's after retiring from their urban jobs. Many expressed their wishes to die at home. Almost always, those who died before retiring were brought back home to be buried at their family cemeteries.

Many times I heard preachers thank God that the deceased family member had been brought home to be buried in the land that he loved. How strange it was that we seemed to feel closer to the land than people from other parts of the country. Being regarded by urban dwellers as backward—and being stereotyped by the nation as ignorant, uneducated hillbillies—only brought us closer together to the land and its people.

Many writers and historians offered reasons for our economic plight. Some said it was the nature of the coal industry, some said it was because wealth had been siphoned off by absentee coal barons and others saw it as simply a matter of local governments not having enough money to provide a good educational system.

It was all these things and more when in 1968 I took a job as Executive Director of the Cumberland Plateau Planning District Commission, a four-county economic development organization designed to bring jobs and a better quality of life to four Southwest Virginia counties. My office was one hundred miles south of Mingo County. Similar organizations were created in all parts of Appalachia to combat the economic plight our people faced.

Through the past thirty years I have managed an agency that has fought to bring our part of Appalachia into the mainstream of American life.

With the help of the Appalachian Regional Commission, the Economic Development Administration and the Commonwealth of Virginia, we have made great strides. In my small, adopted hometown of Lebanon, Virginia, we now have three industrial parks providing jobs for more than 2,000 people and three *Fortune* 500 companies. Similar successes have occurred in all four counties and in all of central Appalachia.

We're building new public water and sewer systems, demanding modern transportation systems, installing broadband fiber-optic trunklines, pushing for better educational tools, cutting-edge medical technology and working each day to bring the quality-of-life items necessary to make life better for the good people of Appalachia.

One of life's greatest joys is learning of someone's family member being able to come home to the mountains to a job not formerly here and made available through our efforts.

So, to all those people in organizations like mine who are working to bring our people home, keep up the good fight. We'll reach the promised land.

Tug Valley Chamber of Commerce Coal House constructed in 1933 with 65 tons of locally mined bituminous coal. The author was Managing Director of the Chamber in 1967-68. (Author's collection.)

Modern day scene of the Matewan Massacre. (Author's collection.)

Welcome to Historic Matewan sign. (Author's collection.)

newspaper's obituary headline

LONG PARTNERSHIP in marriage between "Devil Anse" Hatfield and Levicy Chafin Hatfield started the week after the Civil War began in 1861 and lasted until his death in January 1921 — 59 years. She lived until 1929. Both were of pioneer stock and they had 13 children, the eldest, Johnson (Johnse), being the one who defied the hostility between his family and the Randolph "Ranel" McCoy family by romancing McCoy's daughter, Roseanna. The last surviving child of Devil Anse and Levicy was Willis Wilson Hatfield, who died in 1978 at age 90. (Photo courtesy of Tom C. Chafin)

Devil Anse and wife Levicy Chafin.
(Photo story by Charlotte Sanders, Williamson Daily News.)